AG
AVI : Man

Manifesting Love

Deep Dive into Mythology, Psychology, Astrology, Mystery, and Reality

Dr. Avikshit

gurucool
—PUBLISHING—

i

Published by:

Gurucool Publishing
#102, Sai Krupa Nilayam,
Nagendra Nagar, Habsiguda, Hyderabad – 500 007
Ph: 040–69999200,
E-mail: info@gurucoolpublishing.com

First Edition – 2021

Cover Paintings by: Master Devesh Khanna
                        Miss Naisha Khanna
                        Mrs. Geetanshi Khanna

Dedicated to Lord Krishna

iii

Foreword
by Professor (Dr) Sharda Kaushik

Profile of Dr. Sharda Kaushik

Dr. Sharda Kaushik is Professor and Head, Centre of Management and Humanities, Punjab Engineering College, formerly, Director, Regional Institute of English, Chandigarh. She has worked on various assignments with state governments of Punjab, Haryana, HP and J&K, and has extensively worked with UGC, NCERT, English and Foreign Languages University (EFLU), Hyderabad, British Council, New Delhi, RELO, US Embassy, New Delhi and Ministry of Education, Afghanistan. She has been a member of various Boards of Studies.

She studied for PG Diploma in Teaching English from EFLU. As a British Council Scholar she obtained a Master's degree in Teaching English as a Foreign Language from Reading University, UK, and as a Fulbright Fellow, a Master's degree in Media Communications from Syracuse University, USA. She is a PhD in English from Panjab University, Chandigarh.

Dr Kaushik has been writing for newspapers regularly; having contributed the column 'Mind your Language' in *The Tribune* for a year and has regularly contributed news features to CNN World Report, Atlanta, USA for over four years. Besides the news features she has also made documentaries, one each for Door Darshan (*Kanya ki Kyon ho Bhrunhatya)* and Punjab Police *(Dishaayen).*

Sharda Kaushik has published more than a dozen books with Penguine, Macmillan, Orient Blackswan and Viva among others. She co-authored the book titled *Love in Four Languages* with Late Sardar Khushwant Singh. Apart from that, all her books are prescribed studies in universities, colleges and schools. She has extensively presented papers on Linguistics and Literature at national and international conferences and published some of them in international journals.

Foreword

I am tempted to title the book An Officer and a Gentleman for the simple reason that its protagonist, a naval officer, possesses all the attributes of a gentleman, conducting himself with the courtesy that behoves an officer. However, the title was long taken away by a 1980s Hollywood film. Manifesting Love, the title given to the book by its author, would have certainly claimed the status of its subtitle. The protagonist of Manifesting Love, referred to as Officer, sets out on an expedition of romantic love, which plays a dual role. First, it lays bare the mystery of the emotion and all else we wish to know of romantic love. Second, it validates Officer's self-discovery.

While working on the book titled Declaring Love in Four Languages (DLIFL), which I co-authored with Late Sardar Khushwant Singh, the eminent writer, I examined the depiction of romantic love in poetry, across borders and eras only to realize how little the emotion had changed but for its language of expression. Love, usually, deprives none of its nectar and ecstasy while also spares none of its bitterness and agony. It knows no age or borders just as it debars none for their kind and creed. It entices us with its snare when we least expect it, it acts hard-to-get when we most desire it. A brush with it can be more heavenly than the paradise, a sting from it more deadly than death. Love can make us ride on the waves of hope, high in euphoria and it can drown us in a sea of despair, deep in melancholia.

Melancholy arising from failure in romantic love is hardly a rarity. Shakespeare's plays have numerous characters suffering from one kind or the other of love-melancholy. Melancholy decides to engulf Officer too. In her death, Officer's beloved leaves behind a lover in mourning. But with her departure, she also serves as the catalyst for his journey in search of its meaning.

Officer hardly realizes how complex a phenomenon love is till he meets a series of mentors hailing from all walks of life. In effect, each one enriches him with an understanding of a variety of lovers and with the forms, stages and ways encountered in romantic love, the knowledge domains as varied as astrology, mythology, history, psychology, chemistry, neuroscience, and even social media. Officer must dive into its existence and unfold its mystique, stored in the roots of ancient wisdom and in the explorations of contemporary world. One at a time, Officer acquaints himself with women of substance, each located in exciting surroundings of distant lands. With a deep void within and in the grip of loneliness, he approaches each one, stealthily.

The book is a genre of its own. It uses a modest storyline to narrate how a heartbroken man charts a path towards love; how he progresses from the falling in love stage to its blossoming; how his heart navigates its twists and turns, unique to the situation, unique to the two whose hearts beat together till the realization dawns upon them that they are made for each other. This unassuming storyline, however, makes profound statements. It holds a series of discourse, dense in meaning and invested with minute observations derived from a variety of disciplines. Each covers the complexities of love, myriad shades of life, as the events turn pages in a natural manner.

When love is under review, ranging from the erotic to the sublime, it is next to impossible to not draw upon our ancient past. It may have reference to Lord Krishna, to poet Meera or to apsaras Urvashi and Menaka or, may be, to stories the sculptures of Khajuraho tell. "… no one knows more about love than ancient Indians," remarks one of Officer's counsellors, himself a great storyteller, as he recounts how love is captured in a number of tales in the Mahabharata. I move a step further and align its depiction in ancient history, scriptures and mythology, while acknowledging each one's distinct identity. In DLIFL, when I observed love as an Indian woman, "I felt an intuitive acquaintance with Meera, Radha and even Draupadi, who figure frequently in Hindi love poems and together constitute the collective psyche of Hindu womanhood." The union, separation and the reunion of Shankuntala and Dushyant or Nal and Damyanti can be easily corroborated with the explanations I offered in DLIFL which I quote, "The word prem (love) had a slightly different meaning in Vedic times. Physical compatibility between two individuals was reason enough to enter into cohabitation, which was dissolved the moment the bond began to weaken." When speaking of romantic love and illustrating it with the love Radha and Krishna shared, as depicted in our literature, Jaydev's Geet Govinda cannot be missed out since it reveals many a contour of love. As described in DLIFL, "The song with its erotic overtones blends romance with lust and at the same time carries a religious message through the dalliance of the eternal lovers, Radha and Krishna." Love is seen as religion unto itself.

Another of Officer's counsellors, Dr Sharon Spyke, juggling dual roles, that of the counsellor and the prospective ladylove to Officer, expresses her curiosity, disbelief and reservations on the prudish behaviour of Indians on issues, such as, to be in love with two people at the same time, the approach to divorce, extra-marital relationships, manipulative love and a few others, noticed now and then in the current social norms. On the questions related to love which continue to haunt him, seemingly elementary but with philosophical overtones, she educates him with instances from a range of real life experiences, as well as from research publications, assuaging the tormented soul. Amidst the beauty of nature and shared interests in art, architecture and music, the two are almost on the verge of a long-term commitment but for her ethical concerns over his being her subject.

In one of Shakespeare's quotes on love, the sound of music and the fragrance of flowers are realized as the very manure of love, which accentuate romance in relationships.

If music be the food of love, play on,

… O, it came o'er my ear like the sweet sound

That breathes upon a bank of violets,

Stealing and giving odour. (Twelfth Night)

The haunting love themes of all time romantic classics, Casablanca and Dr Zhivago, as also the opera music at Prague, make an aesthetic appeal to the lovers, deepening the bond. The waters of the river Danube with their mystic appeal, the banks of the river Moskva with the air around filled with dreams, make each riverside Officer's favourite rendezvous. To him, the free-flowing waters of the rivers symbolize freshness, birth and life, hinting at the transitory nature of time, promising hope. On the way to Prague, the sprawling grasslands and the colourful wildflowers complement the mood and the settings frequented by them. The fragrance of lavender, whether emanating from the perfume the ladylove wears or from the scent the lavender flower field bears, binds the motif of love in a single thread.

The conception of fragmented souls, twin flames and soul mates is extensively focused upon in Manifesting Love, illuminating the spiritual facets of the intriguing emotion. The desire for complete surrender and merger with the beloved is an age-old aspiration, found in the Greek, Indian and western literatures alike, each version subject to varied interpretations. In one such myth, the primordial man is slashed by Zeus into two: man and woman. Ardhanarishvara invites a similar understanding. Closer home, as spoke some sages, each one of us was wrenched away from the Brahman at the time of birth. Our intense and at times inexplicable love for the other is the soul's yearning to reunite with the Brahman (DLIFL).

When the poetic nature of love is under review, the mention of social media seems dissonant with its accelerated pace, flippant style and brevity of expression in transmitting messages and in treating even the serious subjects. Well before the launch of social media, almost a decade earlier, the cinema and literary writings, the latter through the centuries, were seen to be celebrating romance, weaved around the separated lovers; the moping lover, the pining beloved, the two suffering from excruciating pain of longing, drowned in an ocean of sadness since they had no means to communicate with each other. The harshest punishment the society could inflict on them was to sever all means of communication. But in the current times, social media offers quick solutions to such barriers with its format of instant gratification. Thereby, it hinders the rise in feelings of helplessness, frustration and anguish, caused by separation that intensifies love and longing.

However, Officer proves the assumption false and finds the love of his life, thanks to the social media.

Manifesting Love can hardly be assigned to a definite readership or select addressees. With its broad sweep on romantic love and its in-depth presentation, it must appeal to one and all among the adult population. Its reference to the knowledge of the earliest Indian times and the scholarship of the modern days makes it a comprehensive work on the complex yet captivating emotion. Manifesting Love is a fascinating voyage of self-discovery, which can mend many a fractured heart and nourish many a parched soul.

Professor (Dr) Sharda Kaushik

Preface

A subject as complicated as 'Love' has intrigued humankind ever since the advent of human life on our planet. Broadly, 'love' has been defined as a form of intense attraction for someone. Every culture and civilisation has its own meaning, definitions, ethics, norms, and behaviour pattern connected with the phenomenon of love. It was definitely not easy to tackle a subject as complicated.

Over a period of time, I believe, 'Love' has appreciably impacted everyone's life. There were amazing findings during my diverse working experience across multiple sectors and nationalities, starting with my stint in the Indian Navy, private sector, and academics. I also realised that a large cross-section of society from all age groups, from childhood to adolescence to adulthood to old age, had some unanswered questions regarding 'Love.' Moreover, everyone's curiosity was unique.

This book has been written to address most of the questions pertaining to 'Love' where answers were possibly not straightforward. I am confident that every reader will surely identify with some or the other sections of the book.

We tend to remember exciting stories narrated to us along with any underlying message those stories attempted to convey. As we all age, we remember a few and forget most of what we learn and experience. Taking a cue from that fact, I decided to present various aspects of the complicated and often misunderstood phenomenon of 'Love' woven in a story so that the reader will find it exciting and effortlessly imbibe the concept as such.

The book is divided into well-connected independent sections, namely Mythology, Psychology, Astrology, Mystery, and Reality of love. Every section can be read independentally also as every topic has been presented as a complete unit.

The story starts with the death of an air hostess in an air crash. She was the love of a Naval Officer. He goes into deep grief. The author narrates the Officer's journey, learning and exploring many aspects related to the sections mentioned above.

In the section 'Mythology,' the Officer learns that Indian mythology is full of tales of love. There are lucid narrations from scriptures of ancient times. The largest epic in the world, 'Mahabharta' itself, has many stories covering a broad spectrum of many love philosophies during ancient times. Some have been touched upon briefly in this chapter. The ancient form of love marriage has been depicted through the story of King Dushyant and Shakuntala. The concept of a lady choosing her husband in a ceremony known as 'Swayamvar' led to King Nall and Damyanti finding each other after years of separation. Until today, no love has been as pure, as reverred and worshiped as Radha and Krishna. Lord Krishna himself had many queens. Draupadi had five husbands. All Pandwas had at least one more wife in addition to Draupadi. Lord Krishna ensured saving the dignity of his great friend Draupadi when her husbands lost her in a game of dice. He also ensured the annihilation of Kauravas in the great war between cousins to keep his promise to Draupadi.

A section, 'Love Hits Hard', is about how an accomplished Professor of Psychology, explains the concepts of infatuation, indications of being in love, romance, thought process, response, care, unending dialogues, and all these connections central to 'Love.' The setting of this section is in Budapest and Prague. The Professor also covers infatuation versus love, Psychology of love, modification in thinking patterns, predictability, eye message, attention, compromise, gratitude, and love's connection with physical health. The Professor keeps the Officer captivated as she explains that love is never lost when it is true through the concept of soul mates and how to comprehend whether you're in love or it's just infatuation. Finally, the Professor educates the Officer on neurotransmitters, physical attraction, and the spirit of 'oneness' when people are in love.

A section, 'Love's Mystery and Society,' is about the Professor's lecture at Stanford University, USA. There she vividly explains how society shapes the way we love. She talks about different kinds of lovers, viz. universal pleasing lover, the manipulative lover, the victim lover, the hesitant lover, and the avoiding lover. She also explains the topics of contemporary love, characteristics of contemporary love, social media communication on the Internet, orchestrated relationships. Professor touches upon love virtues, why traditional love was/is better than contemporary love, also gloving in the prudish behaviour of Indian society.

As the perplexed Officer continues his journey to find the truth about love and suffering, he comes across a south Indian scholar in Tamil Nadu and a north Indian scholar at Hoshiarpur. They explain to him the phenomenon of driving human attachments as per Indian astrology. The Officer learns about Karma, Nadi astrology, and Bhrigu Sanhita. He also learns about secret techniques to ascertain connections of souls, brought out the first time through this book. While these secrets are/were known to great astrologers, they rarely conveyed them out in the open. The author is fortunate to have learned about these in the course of pursuing super-spiritual science.

The author has come across many individuals who feel guilty or anxious that they love more than one person. Most of them are scared to admit it and do not know how to handle it. Many want to know the 'how and why' of it. In the section 'Falling in Love with More Than One Person Simultaneously,' this aspect of love has been amply explained. This section dwells upon how to handle falling in love with more than one individual, emotional monogamy, and elements of such an affair, including polyamory.

The impact of social media on all walks of life cannot be over-emphasised. The section of 'Social Media and

Love' deals with temptations, favorable and adverse effects of social media on relationships, old flames, privacy, and social media rules and relationships.

The section 'Mystery' on 'Reincarnation, Soulmates, and Twinflames' has lifted the curtain on many facets that a typical person always wanted to know. It will be fascinating for the reader to ascertain how to know a reincarnated soulmate. The section deals with the fragmented souls, twin flames, and the signs to recognise whether you've found your twin flame. It deals with the 'feel' like you've known someone your whole life and previous lives. One is sure to be left stunned on acquiring this knowledge as lucidly brought out in this section.

The very practical section on 'Manifesting Love and Happiness' deals with Introduction to 'life coaching,' the Law of Attraction, Affirmations and Self Love, Visualisation, Vibrations and Scripting, power of Gratitude, and Meditation. The write-up explains how to use all these techniques to manifest love in one's life. The chapter is based on my deep research and extensive interactions with the world's renowned life coach. Her actual name is mentioned in the chapter.

Woven in an exciting, naturally flowing storyline, easy-to-understand sections are sure to provide wholesome knowledge and compelling reading on the most potent emotion felt by humankind, which is called 'Love.'

Dr. Avikshit
Cdravikshit@gmail.com

Gratitude

I simply do not have words to express my heartfelt gratitude to those who helped me put this book together. Without their active participation at all stages, completion of the book was not possible. First and foremost is Ms. Prihana Vasishta, a very bright and talented research scholar of Management. She very meticulously helped me to structure and to complete the book.

Commander Sanjay Singh (Retd) read the manuscript in the minutest details, so much so to qualify as co-author. Deep gratitude to him.   Dr. Pooja Chopra, Commander Piyush Sharma (Retd), and Ms. Sargam Bansal offered valuable suggestions. Much grateful to them.

Thanks are due to my young fellow researcher   Jyotish Acharya Meenakshi Sharma, who helped collate very interesting chapter on astrology and brought some secrets of Nadi astrology out to the fore.

Deep gratitude to the world's renowned life coach Ms. Sheena Shah for allowing me to use her actual name for a character inspired by her.

I also acknowledge my kind gratitude to Professor (Dr.) HL Verma, Mr. Rashpal Singh Brar, Dr. Anju Singla, Dr. Kamaljit Kaur, Dr. Anupreet Arora, Dr. Noor Rizvi, Dr. Shivani Gupta, Dr.Sheveta   Bhatia, Mr. Manoj Pathak, Dr. Suriti Goel, Dr. Neha Chaudhary, Rear

Admiral RM Bhatia (Retd), Rear Admiral Rakesh Bajaj (Retd), Rear Admiral Atul Khanna, Surgeon Lt Cdr (Dr.) Rajalakshmi Nott (Retd), Mrs. Shubha Gupta, Mrs. Millie Mishra, Mr. Krishna Kumar Bagri, Dr. Kamna Singh, Ms. Gitanjly Chhabra, Ms. Uma Sharma, Ms. Nidhi Sharma, Ms. Ramneet Kaur, Mrs. Sharmila Dwivedi, Ms. Jennie Bhatt, Mr. Nazir Sawant and Mr. Mukesh Anjaria for their consistent encouragement.

My sincere appreciation and thanks to Dr. Vineet Gera and his publishing house, Gurucool Publishing, for making me aware of various aspects of book writing.

My heartfelt thanks and gratitude to my permanent lucky mascot team, Master Devesh Khanna, Ms. Naisha Khanna, and Mrs. Geetanshi Khanna, for creating numerous paintings and sketches leading to the final cover page/jacket.

My late parents and parents-in-law always inspired me to study different subjects and aspects of life. Their blessings are somewhere evident in this book. Last but not least, I wish to convey my deep gratitude to my wife Anuradha and son Akshiv Avikshit for their constant support. Many thanks to them for standing by me.

Dr. Avikshit

Table of Contents

IV Astrology and Karmik connection of Souls 72

VIII Reincarnation, Soulmates, Twinflames............................... 153

I
Prologue

"Death is certain for the born, and re-birth is certain for the dead; therefore, you should not feel grief for what is inevitable."
Bhagwad Gita. 2.27

The Officer and an Airhostess

1993

She was one of the most beautiful girls he had seen in his life. She was super intelligent. She was a gynecologist by education and qualification and air hostess by choice. No......his mind told him.....she was not on that flight.....that crashed, and everyone on board had died. He had dropped her off at the airport on his motorcycle just a couple of hours ago. He did not want to believe that her flight had crashed into the sea, as he got that news from one of his common friends. He felt giddy. He felt directionless and lifeless. He was stunned beyond words. He wanted to cry, but teardrops would just not flow out of his eyes. He blanked out in disbelief and refusal to accept the truth. Dr Malini Iynger had gone down with the aeroplane.

She belonged to Trichy but was based in Chennai, and he was posted at Mumbai. He was a Naval Officer. A typical well-groomed military man who was deeply convinced that Malini was sent on earth only to be with

1

him. She had decided to join the airline industry as an air hostess due to her fondness for travel, disregarding her profession in the medical stream. Whenever he was not sailing onboard a ship, she would manipulate her roster to fly to Mumbai with a night halt. She would check into an airline-provided hotel and would spend all her time with him. They would see a play, visit US club, take occasional long walks on the seashore, hand in hand. They would often go to the Naval base in Malad (on the outskirts of Mumbai) on his motorcycle to enjoy the private beach within the boundaries of a Naval establishment and relish the privacy of the beach. They would drive on the roads of Madd island while she clung behind him, kissing his neck.

She was a kind of dusky beauty that every writer would have fallen short of words to explain. About five feet and seven inches tall. Her features were like Sage Vedvayasa had explained apsara Urvashi's ravishing beauty and classically built, as ancient sculptures have decorated the temples of Khajuraho. He would never again feel her arms around his neck. He would never smell the lavender fragranced perfume that she so subtly wore as if that fragrance was of her own skin, and he loved that overall feeling. It mesmerized him. He would go in a trance-like state when they made love. Two bodies would melt into each other to become one. And that was their most precious moment.

They were deeply in love. A typical depiction of two bodies and one soul. Those who have researched this subject say that it is possible, that at times soul fragments, and may take rebirth in two or more different bodies. Maybe, after a stagger of very many years. At least one of these souls is likely to recognize their part in another body, wherein they do get attracted very strongly. Even when the Officer and Dr. were physically apart, they would always be thinking about each other all the time. The telepathy would get instant smiles on their faces that emanated straight from their hearts. They would write long letters running up to ten pages at times. Compilation of those letters would have made a fascinating love story. They would tip their postmen heavily for safe and early delivery of letters to them.

The past three years ran across his mind like a flash. They had met at a birthday party of her niece, whose father was his Commanding Officer. The attraction was like a magnet attracts iron, and flowers attract bees. Subsequently, that Commanding Officer was transferred to Delhi. However, the two kept on meeting, and love only grew more and more with time.

Now, his mind felt empty. His emotions and feelings seemed to have dried up. He was in disbelief. He was just not ready to believe that the aircraft in which his lady love would have been smiling as per her duty protocol had ditched into the sea. While he was a strong man, yet all his strength was failing him. His fingers were constantly dialing few phone numbers of the

3

airline office's which he had written in a small pocket diary. That black instrument called 'telephone' was staring at him as his only support. All he wanted was someone on the other end to say that the air crash news was false. His lady love was safe and what he heard was nothing but a rumor.

It was December, a month of reasonably good weather in Mumbai, where most of the year, the weather was annoying for this north Indian Officer due to high humidity. That fateful day, the early morning drive on his motorcycle was again with her as he dropped her off at the hotel next to the airport. From there, she was to be picked up by the airline transport and, after that, report for her duty onboard the aircraft. Her last words were haunting him. 'Take care,' she had told him. She said goodbye with an affectionate smile, removed his helmet, gave him a passionate kiss, and put his helmet back on his head. It made him very happy. He turned his bike with his foot as axis and drove away humming one of the numerous love songs he fondly remembered. This morning he was humming….." I love you more and more as time goes by"….. a great one from the classic movie 'Casablanca.' It was one of their favourite movies. The all-time great film of Hollywood. He remembered how they cherished Indian films too, but most of all, just being together. In the movie hall, they always held hands throughout as they watched the movie.

The sound of a pipe whistle (alert call) by the ship's quartermaster distracted him. He realized that he was standing like a zombie on the ship's quarterdeck (the area on the ship's rear) for more than an hour. Those who had seen him thought that he was there to catch few drags of his favourite cigarette. Little did they know, instead of enjoying his cigarette, he felt smoke was filling inside him, and he was choking as he inhaled it. He had never felt so helpless before. First time in his life, all his senses seemed numb. Nothing was responding, and nothing made sense.

Suddenly, he heard his name being announced on the ship's broadcast, requesting him to go to his superior Officer's cabin. The superior Officer was a kind, bearded, foul-mouthed man. "Where the hell have you been…." he questioned. "Don't you know that you were supposed to be at the fuckin' briefing for the forthcoming fleet exercise 45 minutes ago? Everyone is waiting for you…..no one knows where the hell you were, and there have been frantic announcements for you. My ass is not meant to be torn by Captain for idiots like you. There is panic on board, and Captain is after my life. Now, rush to the ops room. I shall see how to save you, and yes…come back right here the moment all that bloody panic and briefing is over."

Superior Officer's cabin was always stinking as he smoked some cheap brand of cigarette. He was nicknamed as a stinking, foul-mouthed Officer (SFO).

SFO came from an impoverished background in a remote village of Bihar. Son of a peasant, he had an excellent quest for spiritual knowledge. He had good friends that shared the same interest. He would go fifteen kilometers from his home to borrow classic Hindu mythology books from the local Pandit. He had read all Vedas, Puranas, the great epics - Ramayana and Mahabharta many times over. He believed that Mahabharta is the ultimate epic with everything in it, viz action, emotions, erotica, knowledge, spirituality, drama, and everything; and anything that any human being would want to read to understand life as such. He always admired the creator and writer of that epic, namely sage Vedvayasa and Lord Ganesha, respectively. He would often wander between Karamyoga, Gayanyoga, and Rajyoga, which was the best way to Moksha (Liberation from the cycle of re-birth). He would quote Lord Krishna in many conversations. Then, foulmouthed he was. He would abuse in English to show off his rich vocabulary. He had learned English a rather harsh way, invariably getting abused by his superior Officers as he was very lazy. While his superiors hated his laziness, they admired his advice due to his remarkable foresight and brain in analyzing the most complex problem and situations. He certainly had an excellent ability to advise his superiors correctly out of tricky situations many times. They would only ask SFO to change his cigarette brand to something better, as he smoked such detestable smelling ones. The foul smell of the cigarette smoke even wreaked off his uniforms and would not go with the best of washing. Then extremely kind he was. He had a heart of gold. He could just not see anyone unhappy. If he did, he would immediately find a way to cheer them up, even if it meant to give some practical solution based on analysis and correlation of some story or incident of mythological classics.

"I can see that there is something wrong with you today, son. Have you been fucked by a rabbit or spider?" SFO shouted at the Officer. Officer did not reply. He stood in silence and attention even though SFO asked him to ease up. Being Saturday, SFO invited Officer to have a beer with him, as he thought being in a more casual environment could enable him to get the Officer to speak. While the Officer just wanted to be left alone, he had no choice, as it is not customary to refuse an invite of a senior Officer in defence forces. At the bar, Officer was not able to enjoy his drink as he was still lost in oblivion. However, SFO finished his mugful of beer and waved to the steward for a refill. SFO knew that there was something terribly wrong. He could read from the eyes of the Officer that asking him what was wrong may not help. Officer would just not open his heart and mind and rattle out whatever he was thinking or whatever it was that had robbed him of his peace. "How much leave (time-off) have you availed this year?" asked SFO. The Officer replied, "None, Sir." "Don't you think that you need to go home and see your parents?" retorted SFO. "Yes, Sir," replied the Officer. SFO wanted to lighten the mood and said, "You must be having many girlfriends back home waiting for you. In my time, in thirty days of leave, I would date at least ten". SFO had a way to stir up thoughts and emotions in the depths of human beings, in the way he expressed himself even though crass at times. Suddenly, the SFO received a call and stepped out. He asked the Officer to continue to enjoy his drink.

The Officer felt giddy. When he woke up, he was in a ship's sickbay where a medical assistant told him that he was being prepared to be shifted to the hospital on the recommendation of the ship's doctor. The doctor had diagnosed his condition as being in 'severe shock' due to unknown reasons and wanted him to be shifted to the hospital. "Hell no!" the Officer shouted. Hospital is the last thing anyone wanted to be in. He asked the medical assistant to call SFO. He desperately wanted to speak to SFO. When SFO arrived in the sickbay, the Officer almost begged him to get him out of the clutches of the ship's doctor. He certainly did not want to be tied down in the hospital, taking all kinds of medication and being restricted in his movements. Little did he know that SFO was already in discussion with the ship's doctor that the Officer should proceed on leave instead, as he had not availed any since the past nine and a half months. A break from work would be good for the Officer and provide him with some much-needed rest. "I shall convince the Captain to sanction a couple of weeks of leave for you. That's the only way you can avoid hospitalization that too only if that bastard medical Officer agrees". The Officer pleaded, "Please save me from hospitalization. Only if these people knew what has happened to me…"….and that's the cue SFO was looking for. "OK, my son, you prepare to go on leave on one condition, that you will not leave Mumbai with a load on your brain and share whatever has been bothering you. In the meanwhile, I shall tell the department to issue your leave orders." SFO was like a 'midwife.' He knew what was there in every stomach of that ship's crew. " Can I have dinner with you tonight, Sir ?" The Officer requested. SFO immediately agreed and told the Officer to meet him at the club. The club was a nice place to relax. It had its own natural beauty, being right next to the mighty Arabian sea with tables and chairs always neatly laid out on the promenade providing the perfect setting for an evening spent there.

"Oh no…..hell no…..oh my god…..what the hell……" SFO was exclaiming on and on as the Officer narrated what had transpired. Officer was unable to control his pent-up emotions as he spoke. Tears were flowing like a river falling downstream from a high mountain, like a waterfall. Thank god that day some celebrations were going on in the club and there was a massive crowd in and around the dance floor. These two were sitting in a lowly lit corner area. Being low tide, the sea wind had its characteristic fishy smell, yet both were oblivious of it. SFO was shaking his head in dismay and asked. "Do you have a one rupee coin?" The Officer replied. "Yes, Sir." Both went to an old black conventional rotary public phone instrument fixed on a wall next to the club entrance. SFO dialed a number, spoke to someone as the Officer continue to be lost in his own world – in the thought of Dr. Iyengar. On disconnecting his call, SFO told the Officer that Captain had agreed to sanction his leave for 45 days. The Captain was as such a very kind and cordial Commanding Officer. He believed that leave is everyone's privilege, and one must take and make full use of that. Not even once did he ask 'why,' 'what for,' etc.

SFO then made another call, this time with his own one rupee coin. While the Officer continued to be lost in his world of sorrow, SFO booked a flight for the Officer from Bombay to Madras. He took that favor from his friend who worked in an airline ticketing office. Otherwise, it could have been half a day's evolution to get tickets during this time of the year, at short notice. SFO wanted the Officer should meet the next of kin of Dr. Iyenger or someone from her family to bring about some closure. "But Sir, I do not know any of her kin. At least you should have asked me before booking a ticket. What will I do in Madras?" The SFO retorted. "You pull up your bloody socks. Either you die like that girlfriend of yours or hear me out before you object, you idiot." SFO could exhibit empathy, exhort and chastise at the same time.

"You will go to Madras. Your flight is after two days. That's the earliest I could get you through my contact. Consider this flight ticket a gift from me. Before you reach Madras, I shall call up my friend and arrange accommodation for you at the Naval base Officer's Mess. Take only a backpack with you as you will need to do lots of local travelling."

"I want you to understand one thing," he continued, " Just remember that expectations and attachments are two major causes of sufferings and mental instability." The Officer could not comprehend why he was being lectured. He was still numb. Mostly the conversation was going above his head, as he lacked concentration. Nevertheless, he knew that a certain well-meaning action plan had been charted for him, and he certainly trusted SFO. He was probably in for the kind of journey he had never done, imagined, or anticipated. For him, Dr. Iyenger was still looking at him…..with her moist large, dove eyes, like when she finally said 'Take Care' so adoringly with her smiling eyes.

II
Love and Indian Mythology

"I'm certainly not surprised by the passion of the youth for our myths. Mythology is almost a part of an Indian's DNA." Author: Amish Tripathi.

Swami Iyer was a great friend of SFO. He was highly spiritual. Swami had joined the Navy but left prematurely as he thought that defence life was not meant for his spiritual rise. He was from a family of priests from Thanjavur. After leaving the Navy, Iyer did a Ph.D. in religious studies from Annamalai University, Chidambaram. He was fluent in all South Indian Languages, Hindi and English. He understood exactly what was going on when SFO called him up and explained what was required of him. SFO was sure that with his insight, Swami Iyer would be able to drill some peace into the Officer's mind.

Officer got a message that someone with the name of Swami Iyer was waiting for him in the lobby of the Naval Officer's mess, where the Officer was staying. Swami Iyer introduced himself as a friend of SFO. Swami was a handsome bald man with three horizontal lines of white sandal powder on his broad forehead. SFO had requested him to somehow help in reducing the sadness being experienced by the Officer. Swami Iyer was convinced that mythology had all the answers, and

12

he would find the right way to ease the Officer's sorrow. People came to him from all over south India to resolve their conflicts, and he used his astute knowledge of mythology to bring some solace to their lives.

Swami informed the Officer that they would first grab some lunch, after which he would take him to someplace for good coffee. So off for lunch, they went. Officer used to despise eating rice with hands, but Dr. Iyeneger used to love eating with her hands. Very often, she would feed him with her own hands, and the Officer adored that. During lunch at a typical South Indian restaurant, most of them were eating with their hands. When the Officer requested a spoon and fork, he received a frowned look from the waiter.

"How much are you interested in mythology?" Iyer asked the Officer. " Not much," said the Officer. Iyer continued, "How many times have you read Mahabharta?" Now the Officer was getting irritated. "Not even once, but you could say I have read some parts, in comics called 'Amar Chitra Katha.' Iyer again questioned Officer, "Do you know that Adi Parav, the first section of Mahabharta, commences with the love story of Dushyant and Shakuntla?" Officer wanted to run away thinking what kind of a sermon had SFO pushed him in for, but the very mention of the word 'Love' sparked a desire and made him attentive towards the conversation.

Swami Iyer was a great storyteller, and nothing gave him more joy than narrating a story from mythology. " You know that no one knows more about love than ancient Indians."The Officer retorted, "How can you deduce such a fact? " He replied in a typical south Indian accent. " Because I have read scriptures and have done deep research." Swami actually knew many ways to narrate a story according to the listener's temperament. Officer was oblivious to this capability of Swami Iyer. As they finished their lunch, both of them walked out of the restaurant. Officer offered him a cigarette that Swami very graciously accepted. Both of them went to Hotel Taj to have coffee and relax by the poolside.

 Suddenly the Officer saw his watch. It was 1900 hrs. Officer could not believe that he had been listening to mythological stories straight out of Mahabharta one after another since post-lunch. Officer was spellbound and was merrily enjoying such fascinating tales. The lucid storytelling ability of Swami Iyer with the strong underlying current of love had the Officer spellbound. Swami had commenced with the narration of the story of Dushyant and Shakuntla, which was later rewritten by the great poet Kalidas as 'Abhigayan Shakuntalam,' with a slight variation from the original text of Mahabharta. However, Swami Iyer was fully convinced that only 'Gita Press, Gorakhpur'published authentic versions of mythological texts. Therefore, he started with the tale of the name of the country, 'Bharat,' (India), which itself is deeply rooted in love.

So he continued.

Dushyant and Shakuntla

"You know, Maharaja Dushyant, a mighty king of ancient India, while on a hunting spree in a jungle, saw this beautiful girl. Her hair was long and thick. She had washed it and was open drying it with the sway of the mild wind that seemed as though it was blowing with the inherent calm feeling of romance. As she did that, she could sense the presence of someone. She was trying to clear strands of her hair on her forehead, obstructing her vision to see the Maharaja clearly. Her pupils expanded with happiness as there was something in the aura of the mighty king that captivated her. She almost melted with an overwhelming feeling of love when she realized that the Maharaja was also looking at her so lovingly and was possibly mesmerized by her general physique. Her eyes dropped due to embarrassment, and she ran inside the cottage. She straightened her lehenga (long skirt) and adjusted her blouse so as to cover her beautiful, round, firm breasts. She then came out of the door of the hermitage, "Who are you?" she asked " I am Maharaja Dushyant," replied the King. His servants moved forward to get the pretty lady to go back inside the cottage, but the king waved them to stop. "Whose ashram is this, and who are you so beautiful lady? " he asked with all the tenderness. " Rishi Kanwa's, and I am his daughter," she replied. The Maharaja said, "I am smitten by your beauty, dear lady. I am unable to take my gaze away from you." The lady blushed but continued to look at him.

Her name was Shakuntla. Sage (Rishi) Kanwa had brought up Shakuntala after her mother, Apsara Menaka, abandoned her. History has it that Menaka was deputed by Dev King (King of the Gods) Indra to break the penance of Sage Vishwamitra, as Indra felt insecure about Sage Vishwamitra and saw him as a competitor for the Kingdom of Heaven. Menaka could seduce Sage Vishwamitra, break his penance, and thus Shakuntala was born from their union.

After niceties and protracted wooing, Shankuntala agreed to be the wife of King Dushyant. However, Shakuntala had one condition that only her son born out of their union should ascend the throne, and to that, the love-smitten King readily agreed. They got married secretly. When Sage Kanwa returned, they informed him about what had transpired between them. Sage Kanwa approved of their union and told the couple that their kind of union was acceptable as 'Gandharva Vivah,' a marriage where no one's consent is necessary.

 After enjoying a few days of marital bliss, Maharaja left, promising to return soon to take back his lady love and introduce her as a queen to the populace of his kingdom. After many years, when the Maharaja did not return, Shakuntala decided to go to the palace. She walked up to the king, chairing a meeting with his ministers and reminding him of his promise. Initially, King Dushyant feigned ignorance being sheepish of how he could indicate the truth to the people of his Kingdom. However, after some melodrama, he agreed to take Shakuntla as a queen.

Nall and Damayanti

Swami knew how and where to change the pitch. By now, they had consumed a jug of coffee and half a packet of cigarettes each. Time was flying by. Officer requested him to continue. This time Swami changed his style of narration and said. "You know that no bond can ever be more robust than love. Love is of many types!" He then narrated another story.

During ancient times, King Nall and his beautiful queen Damayanti were exiled into the forest by his brother as Nall lost his entire kingdom in a game of gambling. Subsequently, even queen Damyanti was abandoned in the woods, scantily clothed. She faced many unruly elements but somehow reached her father's house. Her father was also the king of his region. Her parents were furious learning about what had happened to her. They would often try to convince her to remarry. Damayanti was sure of the love of her husband. Despite all the hardships that she was left to face, she felt fate separated them but was confident that Nall would indeed find her one day. She also pressed some spies into service to locate Nall. In the meanwhile, Nall, in disguise, had taken up a job of a charioteer in another kingdom.

Being an astute person, he was made the King's charioteer as he was also an expert in handling chariots and horses. One day his King received a message that

17

Damayanti's father had organized a 'swayamvar.' In this ritual, the lady would choose her husband from the eligible ones for her marriage. In this case, Damayanti was to choose her second husband, as the first husband was not traceable. Nall's employer king decided to participate. Nall was highly disturbed thinking as to why Damayanti's father had organised the swayamvar. He always believed that she was much in love with him. Therefore wondered, how could she even think of remarriage? These thoughts made Nall even more restless.

Nevertheless, time was short to cover such a considerable distance for the swayamvar's venue. Nall selected the best horses to pull the chariot. Once he took the reins, he steered the chariot in the direction of his wife's father's kingdom. As he sped the chariot, his present master king randomly mentioned the number of leaves on one particular branch of a tree. Nall pulled the horse's reins and wanted to check the validity of King's ability to count. The king was a master in this art, including in the art of gambling.

Seeing Nall slowdown, the King pleaded with Nall to hurry up lest they should miss the deadline. Now was the time for Nall to assert what he wanted, so he said, " I shall drive you to the palace on time provided you teach me the science of numbers and gambling, as I take you there." He added, "In return, if you want, I shall teach you all about horses." The king was mighty pleased and agreed. And as Nall steered the galloping horses, the King educated Nall. Skillful Nall used all his skills to ensure they were in Damanyanti's father's kingdom on time. People all over the kingdom were in awe and talked about the great charioteer who had covered such a significant distance in record time. When the news trickled to Damayanti, she smiled to herself; she knew that there was only one person in the whole world who could cover that distance on a chariot this fast. She was sure of her herself. Ultimately Nall and Damayanti were in arms of each other. Two bodies became one soul.

Said Swami, 'Unless you are sure of yourself, you cannot be sure of anything else." He smiled after making this significant point. He also told the Officer that he would explain the phenomenon of souls, bodies, flames, etc. Officer nodded his head vigorously in agreement and thanks as he smiled.

"Do you know that Pandwas were either sleeping with most desirable women or fighting?" Swami laughed as he said that with a typical south Indian accent.

"I also wish to tell you that multiple varieties of love, unions, and marriages are there in our mythology—no one used to mind what we call unorthodox or unconventional nowadays."

"What do you mean by that ?" asked the Officer, and Swami Iyer replied. "I am sure you know that all Pandwas were married to Draupadi, but individually they also had their wives." Officer laughed aloud and said. "Such lucky princes. Here I am drowned in the love and thoughts of only one, how did they manage?"

As he said that, he remembered Dr. Iyenger, he sank back into his very low mood. He thought the only way he could pull himself out of that low-spirited mood was if Swami Iyer continued his talk. Iyer was brilliant. He could make out something was bothering the Officer but could also clearly tell that Officer was losing focus and was fatigued. So, Swami made an excuse of being tired but promised to see the Officer the next day after breakfast. The Officer acknowledged the plan and went back to his room, where he did not even change into his sleeping pajamas and hit the sack. The Officer got up in the middle of the night with the nightmare that he was also in the plane that crashed. He was sweating. He lit a cigarette. He took out a picture of Dr. Iyenger from his wallet, kissed that, and somehow went back to sleep.

It was 1000 hrs when he woke up with a headache. He fetched a newspaper from under his cabin door. As he opened the newspaper, he saw a smiling picture of Dr. Iyenger in the obituary section. Unfortunately, he did not have the guts to read what was written.

The Officer got ready, carried the paper, and rushed to the Naval Officers' lobby for lunch to join Iyer. With the paper folded in a way where Dr. Iyengar's obituary could be seen, the Officer exchanged an unspoken glance with Iyer about her. "Yes, I have seen that," said Iyer in his typical south Indian accent. While having lunch, they had decided to do some nonstrenuous sightseeing. They also decided to go for the thirteenth day Pooja (prayer meet) at Dr. Iyenger's house. It was evident that Officer was being taken charge of by Iyer directly and SFO indirectly. So they headed out post-lunch as per plan.

Arjun's various marriages

As they walked on Mahabalipuram beach, the Officer requested Iyer to narrate something interesting from mythology. Officer always found those stories so exciting and marveled at the writers. Swami agreed and told the Officer that he would say to him about Arjun, the sharpest of the Pandwas.

"Draupadi was won over at a swayamvar by Arjun. However, following some dharma (religious) issues and miscommunication within the family, she was married to all five brothers. A principle existed between five Pandwas brothers that no one will intrude a space of one brother if he was with their shared wife, Draupadi. Unfortunately, Arjun had to intrude the space to fetch his weapons, required to help a citizen, as those were lying at the same place where his brother Yudhishter was with his wife. Following the breach of the code of conduct by Arjun, he had to proceed out of his kingdom on 12 years exile. During that exile, he married Ulupi, a serpent princess, who confessed to having an intense liking for him. Then there was this Manipuri Princess Chitrangada, a divinely beautiful woman with whom Arjun fell in love. Her father allowed marriage because a son of their wedlock would be made king of Manipur, to which Arjun ready agreed. He stayed in Manipur state for three years and left once a son was a little older.

21

Subsequently, Arjun took a fancy for Krishna's sister Subhadra. Krishna, as astute he was, advised Arjun to kidnap his sister and elope with her. However, Krishna knew very well that his clan would not agree to this alliance. So Krishna, with his great mind, held back his clan, including his brother Balram from attacking Arjun. The most amazing part is that none of these women insisted on living with their respective husbands throughout their life. That was so amazing and strange.

"Lucky men," joked the Officer. "Yes, yes, and their children supported Pandwas during the great war of Mahabharata. Like the role of Ghatotkach, born due to love between Bhim and Hidimba, sister of demon Hidimba. In fact, his bravado was such that Karan had no option but to use his most potent weapon on him. Karan had kept this weapon safe, with the intention to only use it for killing Arjun. With Karan having lost his power weapon, Arjun could kill Karan with the help of an intelligent move facilitated by Krishna.

Now, this is where it gets interesting, said Iyer.

Eighth Patranis of Krishna and Radha

"Lord Krishna is one of most revered Gods in the Hindu religion. He was the ninth avatar of Vishnu. While giving the all-time greatest and famous discourse to Arjun, as described in the epic, 'Bhagwad Gita,' Krishna openly declared that he was God and will guide his followers towards salvation. He also had an enormous female fan following in his human form, and all of them wanted to be close to him. While growing up in Mathura, Vrindavan, and Gokul, Krishna's lady love was Radha. Elder to him, by 11 months, their relationship could be considered two bodies and one soul. In fact, she has always been held in much higher esteem as Krishna's lover than any other of his eight wives.   Rukmini, Satyabhama, Jambavati, Kalindi, Mitravinda, Nagnajiti (also called Satya), Bhadra, and Lakshmana (also called Madra) were Krishna's wives. Still worshipping Radha has been considered more sacred than worshipping Krishna alone. It is said that if you worship Radha, you get additional blessings from Krishna. Krishna and Radha had one soul. The history is saturated with various anecdotes of these two. So much music, dances, dramas, and music have been created on love between Radha and Krishna. They are revered and have a special place in Hindu mythology.

To escape attacks from Jarasandh, the King of Magadh, who wanted to kill Krishna, Krishna had to leave Mathura, his birthplace, in north India. He established his kingdom at a western Indian seashore in a place called Dwarka in Gujarat. Once Krishna left Mathura, he never went back. He never met Radha again. Yet, the most prominent example of love in Indian mythology is that of Radha and Krishna. Most Krishna temples in India have Radha along with him. Radha gives Lord Krishna a kind of completion. There has been no mention of any physical intimacy between the two in any of the scriptures. Sublime love was the only aspect discussed. Their union has been considered highly noble. Both were complete with each other, even without ever being together. They showed the world the exact meaning of love, where being complete with each other through their souls was key.

Officer loved this story, his eyes shone, and he asked Swami. "So, do you mean to say that marriage is not the final culmination of two people in love?" "Of course not," retorted Swamy Iyer. Officer knew that Radha and Krishna were worshipped together. But, since he was predominantly educated in a western environment, such details or aspects of his religion were not known to him, nor was he interested at the time. For him, life meant just being with Dr. Malini Iyenger. He often wondered why she was always discouraged from talking anything about her family. Frankly speaking, he too was not much interested in family affairs. If any topic cropped up by mistake, she would lovingly evade the issue either by shutting him up with a soulful kiss or tickle or a loving caress on the back of his neck. That was enough to make him lose control and forget any family topic.

Friendship of Krishna and Draupadi

"Do you know who were best of friends in ancient India? " Asked Swami Iyer with a grin. By then, the Officer was exhausted with so much information, but he wanted Swami Iyer to go on and on. Though exhausted to death, Officer was never so fascinated before, and he was comparing his love with the love of all these heroes Iyer was talking about. While he was amazed to know about the love of Radha and Krishna, he tried to compare his own love for Dr. Iyenger.

"Do you know who Draupadi called for help when being molested by cousins of her five husbands?" "I know that," retorted the Officer. "That was Lord Krishna." Iyer questioned, "But why Lord Krishna? Why not her so powerful five husbands?" Officer said something that instantly brought a smile on the face of Swami. "Her husbands must have been impotent!" The Swami said, "Good try. However, the fact is even though they had lost the kingdom and the queen, the dignity of Draupadi was never at stake. So how could they even see their wife being molested? It was the greatest of relationships between Draupadi and Krishna that saved the dignity of Draupadi." Swami continued, "Not only her dignity on that day, but Krishna also ensured that Draupadi was in a happy state of mind and remained fearless. He also ensured that all wishes of Draupadi came true, whether it was Pandwas punishing Kauravas or punishing Ashwat-thama." Officer had never heard or thought of this before. Moreover, Swami also told him that once Krishna had ensured that Draupadi was not subjected to embarrassment when many hungry Brahmins gathered at her cottage during Pandwa's exile period. There was no food in the house, but with the bliss of Krishna, they all felt satiated.

Officer was exhausted, body tired, but still wanted Swami Iyer to go on and on. Officer was particularly interested in knowing how Krishna's friendship with

Draupadi could pacify Draupadi when she was devastated with Ashvat-thama killing all five of her sons and brother in one go. As the greatest karma yogi, Swami told Officer that Krishna made all efforts to avert any war. However, he did not stop it beyond a point, as Draupadi wanted to see the end of Kauravas, who molested her, in front of all elders. For that, Krishna promised Draupadi that her insult would be avenged. However, Krishna, with his excellent understanding, ensured that happened without lifting a weapon. Swami went further in saying that Krishna also facilitated that Draupadi gave a lesson to one of his wives, Satyabhama, when they called on Pandawas at their exiled place. Therefore, Swami pointed out that it is essential to understand that Krishna and Draupadi were deeply attached as friends. She would share all her joys and sorrows and trusted Krishna much more than anyone in the whole universe. Krishna gave her utmost respect and care. He ensured that whatever Draupadi wished was manifested. It was such a beautiful and pure bond.

"OK, who was the father of Pandawas ?" Officer loved this south Indian accent of Iyer. Unfortunately, the Officer did not know the answer.

"You know that in olden times, sex without love was justified to produce children. It was considered mystical! Like children of Kunti were born between with her union with devatas (God) namely; Dharamraj, Vaayu, and Indra after marriage; and from Suraya devata (Sun

26

God) before marriage." "So interesting," grinned the Officer. "They were Yudhishter, Bhim, Arjun, and Karan, respectively." "OK, but I understand that there were five Pandwas ?" "Yes, you uneducated Officer" first time, Iyer was irritated by the scant knowledge of the Officer. Swami always believed that the education system in India should include the study of Sanatan dharma, being the oldest in the world. "Two brothers Nakul and Sahadev were born to the second wife of Raja Pandu from a union of their mother, Madri, with two devas Ashwani Kumars. Hence three sons of Kunti born with the knowledge of her husband and two sons of Madri are Pandwas." When the Officer asked why Pandu could not produce his own, he learned from Iyer that Pandu would have died on having sex with either of his wives due to a curse. The Officer was shocked at learning these details of the Pandwas.

Greater Shock

Iyer had insisted that the Officer must attend the thirteenth day Pooja (prayer) ceremony for the last rites connected with the demise of Dr. Iyenger. It was being held in a temple at Sriman Raghwan road, Madras. So both of them went to that place.

SFO had already briefed Iyer on what to expect when the Officer eventually learned that Dr. Iyenger was married at 18 with her maternal uncle. In south India, that was the tradition and was followed widely. However, she was not happy with that union. Hence she went to Vellore to complete her MBBS (graduate in medicine and surgery) and then MD (Masters, for being a Medical Doctor). However, she decided to pursue working for the airline industry instead and thus joined Air India as a hostess in due course.

Sure enough, the Officer fainted when he learned of her past. In his fainted and exhausted state, Iyer escorted him out of the ceremony, put him in a car, and brought him to his house, where his doctor friend was waiting to look at him.

III
Love hits hard

"Then it hits you so much harder than you ever
thought it would."
Unknown

Budapest: 2005

"University of Budapest?"   "University, yes! I am here
to attend the conference for four days," she said. Officer
did not know why he decided to strike a conversation
with this 40 ish, gorgeously beautiful white woman. He
had landed a night before and, after heavy breakfast,
booked this walking tour. His intention was to explore
the beautiful city of Budapest. He was in the town for
some quality solitude. She didn't even look at him. Yet,
something was compelling him to strike a conversation
with her. She was wearing glasses, those that curtailed
the glamour of her beautiful green eyes. She was more
interested in listening to the story narrated by the
walking tour guide, explaining that Buda and Pest were
two different cities connected with an elegant bridge.

She ignored the Officer during the walking tour, and he
wondered why. He still wanted to communicate with her
somehow. He was a good Officer with high self-esteem,
and being given the cold shoulder was something he
could not fathom. "Ma'am, it seems you are ignoring me
just because of my skin color, or is there any other

29

reason," asked the Officer. She looked at him from the top of her glasses that seemed wide lensed glasses. " Who are you, Sir? I don't even know you; where is the question of ignoring you?" said she. "And please don't speak mindlessly. I do not understand why you brought in the color angle. I do not interact with people who I don't know or with whom I don't feel like speaking with."

Now Officer was irritated to the core. He was angry and disturbed for no apparent reason. She was right, he thought. She did not even know him to ignore him. On completion of the tour, the Officer came back to the hotel. As the Officer lay in bed, reminiscing the morning, he shook his head in a disgusting smile, thinking of the interactions, and then dozed off.

It was 1930 hours when he made his way down to the bar from his hotel room post a good nap. As he seated himself on a bar stool, the Officer saw a familiar face on the adjacent bar stool. The gentleman in him could not stop asking her, "Can I request the pleasure of having a drink with you, as my invite." and he gave her the cutest smile. She smiled back in acceptance of this invite. Both got up and sat at a table in the corner of that bar. "I love to stay at this place. I do not like to mingle around in the evenings with all those boring people at conferences," said she, as she started sipping her Campari. She somehow seemed to love that drink, as there was a sparkle in the eye when she sipped it. She then said that she liked the intellectual side of those conferences but moved around independently and relished every moment in her way once her sessions were over.

Dr. Sharon Spike was her name. She was a double doctorate, a celebrated and highly distinguished Professor ofPsychology. She had in-depth knowledge of relationships and human behaviour. The intellectual circles would queue up to listen to her, and people of all ages would wait for months to meet her on appointment. She kept her personal life a closely guarded secret and would neither socialize nor date anyone from her work circle.

She had travelled from Oslo, Norway, where she was a well-established Professor in a premium University. She was considered an authority on the psychology of relationships and also well known in the literary world. Students of the Psychology department of her University would make a beeline to be a part of courses that she taught every semester, for her teaching and insight into worldly affairs was exemplary.

Dr. Spike was actually invited to attend this conference at the University. She would accept such invites twice every year. She would be invited to different cities across the globe and combine three weeks of leave to make it a months trip. She was a passionate traveler, and during her travels, her step-sister would look after her small daughter. Her daughter was born as a result of a week's stay with a fifty-five year old clerk working at the nearby store. He was a good man and had taken exceptional care of her when she fell ill during her one of solo sojourns at Alancate, Spain. Unfortunately, his life was short-lived, and he passed away due to a heart attack. That was five years ago.

Seeing places, museums, art galleries, monuments, attending concerts, and once in a while having good sex only, if she really fancied someone, could also be on the cards. For her, kindness and compassion were the greatest virtues. An excellent male's deep voice would also attract her much more than sheer looks and typical six-packs that she hated.

"Don't you get bored traveling alone?" the Officer asked her as he sipped his local Hungarian whiskey, and she continued to sip her Campari with soda. There was loud laughter from her as she found that question funny. For her, it was the other way round. A bliss of time. Solitude was bliss. She always went back more learned, enriched, and churned out at least two high-quality papers for reputed Journals following every travel. That not only got her fame but also huge clientele as a 'Relationship Counsellor and Coach.'

After dinner, he escorted her to the room. Said goodbye with a gentle hug and a light peck on her cheek. They had planned to move around together the next day after lunch as she had a paper presentation during morning hours. Officer could charm her enough to agree to bunk the second half of the session to be with her. He had learned that she was a great psychologist.

Officer expected some insight into questions that had been haunting him since that earth-shattering day of hearing the news of the air crash. In fact, he would still go into a cocoon whenever he thought about that. Obviously, Dr. Iyenger's demise had everything to do with that. Hence the Officer had great hope that maybe he would get the answers he had been seeking for so many years through Dr. Spike. The questions had plagued the Officer even though he had gotten married to a lovely, homely, highly educated girl who had a job in a nearby school where they lived not to get bored when the Officer was away.

It's been so many years now, but he still had not come to terms with her loss. The very thought of the aircraft crashing still gave him shivers. He wanted to know the reason for his strong attachment to Dr. Iyengar. He wanted to understand how two persons could be so strongly attached? What was that phenomenon called love? Why is it such a strong emotion? How the brain controls it? Someone had mentioned the term ' infatuation' back then in 1995. What was that? Etc etc. etc. Will he ever be able to love again? Though he would tell his wife so many times that he loved her, he knew that was not wholly true in his heart of heart. He respected her a lot. He cared for her a lot. He would provide anything that she asked for. But was he in love with her? He honestly could not say yes to that from the core of his heart. He adored his two children, a boy, and a girl, and thought of his wife as a good and great lady too. The Officer was actually deputed to Berlin on some official duty, and he had taken few days off from work to visit a couple of places and chose Budapest first at the insistence of SFO.

Dr. Spike waited in the lobby as the Officer arrived precisely at the scheduled time of 1300 hrs. It was 19 degrees celsius and a sunny day. They booked an eight-hour cruise on the river Danube. She told the Officer, "This river always fascinates me as it traverses through so many countries and historical places and also has some mystic appeal."

As the barge made its way through the Danube, Officer began to narrate the story and his times with Dr. Iyengar. Dr. Spike heard the story with great intent and a loving smiling. However, the Officer's voice would choke up with emotions now and then. "That's fine. That's OK. What's so new in that? While in Bombay, she wanted to be with you to steal moments of happiness that she deserved and was not getting. You gave her that mental and physical stimulation," Dr. Spike told the Officer.

He could see empathy in Dr. Spike's beautiful eyes as he completed the story of his love. She told him that she could fully understand what he was going through, but he would have to eventually release Dr. Iyenger and accept reality! He felt a strange relief as she hugged him, as his tears rolled out. She was sort of taller than him. She put her arms around him in a way to make him rest his head on her shoulder and said, "Did someone not tell you what a big, cute, and rare specimen you are?

Why are the events of the past haunting you so much? Why have you made your life hell?" she asked as she released his head from her shoulder to look him in the eye. His tears had made her honeydew complexioned shoulder all wet. "My heart and soul are not at rest. Every day in the morning, I get up in agony", he said. "Do you really wish to know about love and infatuation and all those phenomenon ?" She asked him plainly. "So many people tried, but I never understood. They use such high-sounding words with complex theories that I cannot comprehend." She said, "I do not know who you have asked or what they told you. I am asking you simply, do you want to know about love or infatuation." Officer could see some sense of authority in her voice and immediately nodded his head in affirmation. He told her he would be back. He then went across the barge deck in which they were cruising and fetched two water bottles for both of them. They sat on a bench along the edge of the deck, enjoying the gentle breeze, and she started……..

Love hits hard

"Love is the hardest hitting weapon ever known to mankind." With a heartful laugh, Dr. Spike commenced talking to him. She loved to lecture, and he was so mesmerized by her persona and that he just wanted her to talk. The intent and innocence of the Officer made Dr. Spike also develop some kind of affection for him, and it is how she decided to educate him. Dr. Spike wanted to ease out many years of pent-up emotions from the Officer's mind. She also instinctively knew that her routine Psychological counselling techniques might not work. As the Dr. felt unique emotions for the Officer, she had decided to explain the phenomenon until the Officer was at peace and satisfied. She also did enjoy his company as the Officer was an excellent conversationalist. Even SFO found the Officer's personality to be engaging. He had a great sense of humor. Other than the blank left in his life by Dr. Iyenger, he was a man with a charming personality. Dr. Spike considered him to be a thorough gentleman. Not even once did he try to touch her, which was one quality, she adored in any male. She always wanted to control and approach any situation herself, even if it was sexual attraction. She was very comfortable in his company and was ready to impart lessons of love to this Officer.

Officer told her that he was a good listener. So, she held his hand, caressed it with another one, and said, "You know…. What I am going to tell you will help you. So, I want that you better listen to me attentively, as I am also a serious teacher." So, she started.

"When it comes to humanity, love is peculiar. Sometimes, it could be pleasant and clear. Other times it may not be clear and full of dark holes. Have you ever asked yourself whether you're really in love with someone? Yes, I guess we've all been there. But, even though you may not know what the feeling is, there is a way actually to figure things out. There are ways to decipher whether you have actually fallen in love with someone. When you visualize yourself in any of these emotions that I'll be sharing with you, then the chances are that you are in love, and these feelings will drive you to do things that you have never imagined. They will make you feel an unknown level of happiness, and you will see life differently. So, let's look at the first one." She said with a straight face as if taking a class for postgraduate students.

Indications of being in love

Thoughts

"When you are in love with someone, the person will always live in your thoughts. Like, literally. When they are already in your heart, it will be hard for their memories to leave your mind. You will not stop thinking about that person. Any situation or a thing you see that is similar to the one you saw with the person will quickly remind you of them. These thoughts will always come involuntarily, and sometimes you'll find yourself missing the person so much that you want to meet with them right away. Also, most of your actions at that moment will be motivated by that special being. In the process, you may even change to blend with them. Now, if this is you, then that's love."

Response

"Another way to know when you are in love is that you'll begin seeking approval of the person before taking certain actions. Actions or decisions that you normally would have taken by yourself. Now, you'll always be waiting for their answer. And, as you wait for them to respond to whatever you asked them, your

37

heartbeat will become faster, and that may cause you to become impatient. Why? Because you just want to hear from them right away, and them keeping you waiting is already making you anxious and restless. Sometimes, in such cases, you may even find yourself getting angry at the person. All these are signs indicating that you're already in love with the person. Hearing from them will feel exhilarating. You might even blush uncontrollably and speak of having mind-blowing feelings."

Officer was in a different world, as she explained. He was feeling ecstatic. He remembered feeling those emotions with Dr. Iyenger as their love blossomed.

Professor was going on and on, and from her experience of so many years, she knew that Officer was spellbound and in a state of extreme euphoria.

Professor continued,

Next-Level Experience

"This is one of the clear signs of falling in love. Yes, you indeed have a sensation in you, a strong feeling of eagerness almost like passion and a fire roaring to spread. These sensations, however, occur when you know that you will have an encounter with that special person. There is nothing in the world that will be more important than being with them at that moment. As a result, you will feel both excitement and anxiousness while anticipating that moment. How serious does this get? Well, you will gladly forfeit watching your favorite game or show just because you want to spend time with the person. And no matter how much time you spend together, you'll always feel like it's never enough. When you feel this way towards someone, then the chances are that you're already in love with the person."

Romantic

"Another way to know if you've fallen for someone is that you randomly become a more romantic person. Put differently. You'll start finding more creative ways to act and look romantic when with the person. You'll do everything possible for that person to be surprised. This could include gifting them something they had told you they wanted, or it could be breaking your usual routine just to make them feel loved. Over time, doing this will become a part of your life, and you'll always invent or become creative."

Listening to her, the Officer thought, "How does she know what all I have gone through," as he tried holding her hand that she shook away. Professor Spike did not like to be disturbed when she spoke. However, the Officer was pleasantly amused at her knowledge, and she continued....

Unending Dialogues

"When you are with someone you love, you'll never want your conversation with the person to end. You may even notice that it always feels as if time is running faster than usual only when you are with them. No, time isn't running faster than usual; you're just in love. This is because you just want the talk between you two to last forever. You don't even want it to end. It gets overwhelming, you love it, but time still flys by. You wish you get an extension. Instantly, all their interest become yours too. If they love talking about sports? You instantly become interested in sports. If they talk about shopping, you love to hear about that. Anything spoken is fine as long as you get more time. That's love."

Care

"When you are in love with someone, all of a sudden, you'll start to have this huge desire to protect the person. So you'll be willing to help and support them with everything they need. You'll start worrying about things like their food, work environment, getting enough rest, and whether they're feeling good, emotionally speaking. Put differently, their well-being and comfort will become your priority. And since they have become your priority, you'll start to feel like you are in your best time and best shape whenever you're with them. That is, their presence will bring you joy, and when you guys happen to be apart, you'll start missing them almost instantly."

Officer remembered that Dr. Iyenger would ensure to get him anything even if he mistakenly talked about liking something. She would fly international very often. She would browse through custom shops just to pick up something for the Officer to surprise him. That gave her immense satisfaction, but all the Officer wanted was her to be back as he was always missing her.

As the cruise continued, people were wining and dancing all near the bar in the center of the barge. However, Dr. Spark continued to educate the Officer. She was oblivious to anything when she talked on this subject.

She continued….

Change

"Last but not least, when you're in love with someone, you'll start changing or modifying things inside you. This could include denying to them that you're in a relationship, thus claiming to be single. Or, you can start smelling nice just to make them like you more. You'll do this because you have a soft spot for them, and you don't want to let it go. Although, you should always smell nice at all times."

Now, here is what I need you to know. Said the Professor, "There is a very thin line between love and what we call infatuation. Let me use my colleague's case study here. Back then, in the university, he used to lead a very quiet and reserved life. This behaviour continued for years until one day. Then, he came across this girl. Her name was Sahana. It was love at first, sight; at least so he thought. Two days after getting to be her friend, he already had adrenaline rushes, and he began having imaginations of all kinds with her and about her in his head. To cut the story short, two weeks after getting to be her friend and having the chance to kiss her and be intimate with her, never materialized, as his urge

41

had dwindled. Why? He loved her, right? No, he didn't love her. While it seemed that he couldn't stop thinking about her and even tried his best to make her happy, it was all an infatuation. So, with that being said, what is infatuation? And what is love?"

"Wow!" exclaimed the Officer, almost pleading with the Professor to continue promising to fetch two glasses of local Hungarian wine. Professor agreed, thanked him for the wine, and continued…..

Infatuation Vs. Love

"How can you tell if someone's just fascinated with you or if they like you and vice versa? Similarly, how can you tell if you're experiencing infatuation in your own heart? To know this, you must first understand these two feelings to decipher whether you're confusing one for the other. So let's first start with infatuation." Dr. Spike spoke like a seasoned teacher, entirely in control, with great poise and a subtle smile.

The Officer was hooked on brilliant explanations from the Professor, who knew her subject well. No jargon, no heavy words, nor definitions, just simple logic to pitch her explanations and knowledge at an appropriate level so that her Officer student understand was able to grasp what she wanted to say.

She continued…..

Infatuation

"Infatuation is very similar to idolatry. It is when your feelings aren't rooted in the truth of the relationship. By that I mean, you've created false ideas or things you just really don't know about this person. You've created them in your mind, and now you're infatuated with this perfect idea of somebody that isn't rooted in reality. One basic definition of infatuation is an intense but short-lived passion or admiration for someone or something. Like in my colleague's case, it only took two weeks for his feelings to fade away because it was infatuation in the real sense. This is why you don't want this in a relationship because it's a feeling that may be intense initially but then vanishes pretty much just as fast as it got into you. Now, love is the opposite of that."

Love

"Love, unlike infatuation, is not like an on/off power switch. Things are not rushed, it grows over time. True love takes time, and that's why it endures until eternity when built on the right foundation. It doesn't fade in a month or two; it only grows stronger and deeper as the day goes by. Within the Bible, for instance, love is sacrificial. Put differently, that's when you're doing something sacrificial for the benefit of another person. For example, in John 15:13, Jesus said there was no higher love than to lay down one's life for his friends. He made the ultimate sacrifice; therefore, he showed the ultimate expression of love. So, that's what love is all about. It's about commitment, serving from the depth of one's heart. It's not about faking, idolizing, and being infatuated. Instead of idolizing and making up unrealistic imagery about the person in your head, love is real. Even when they don't deserve the high intense love, love doesn't care. When there is love, it will conquer, and things will move on just fine. Unlike infatuation, there is a great deal of psychological fact one needs to know about love. This is because love itself is so deep that you might get lost in it if you don't know your way around it. So, what are these psychological facts that you should know when talking about love?"

The Officer thought, how could she talk so much? How does she know so much? Officer was a plain graduate engineer in the Navy and temperamentally did not like academics or anything associated with that. He was fond of games, adventure, long drives on his bike, and sports. However, since the air crash, he was always interested in any conversation that had some connection with love. The pain inside him was as still as fresh as that fateful day.

Psychology of Love – Few things

She was thoroughly enjoying lecturing this Officer. He was listening in rapt attention, looking straight into her eyes, barely blinking so as not to miss her expressions. He never knew that someone could explain the phenomenon or interlinking aspects of love in such simple words. At times, he felt her subtle breath on his extended forearm while she just continued with her intellectual talk.

Modification in Thinking Pattern

"When you fall in love, it changes the chemistry of your brain. Now, not only does love release hormones, but love also creates new emotions. It also inspires your brain to give up bad habits. By that, I'm referring to addictive behaviors. So, let's say you're a chain smoker. Once you fall in love, it's easy for you to be distracted from this habit because most of the time, the love for your partner will often take up a major part of your brain. Also, if they tell you to stop, it's easy for you to do so because you love them and wouldn't want to disappoint them just because of some bad habit. Therefore, however difficult, you will find yourself working on getting rid of the addiction."

"Passionate love diminishes your reactivity to addictive behavior. Put differently. Love is so distracting that your brain stops craving your bad habits. Like I just said, if you ever want to change your bad habits, do it at the beginning of a relationship. Love will make it much easier to let go of those, as all you want is to be in Love and nothing else!"

He was listening spellbound, and she continued ……

Eye Message

"When someone loves you, you'll see it in their eyes. How? Let me explain. So, let's say you're having dinner with your better half. Do they spend the entire date looking around the room, or do they spend it staring at you? When you look at someone you love, your brain releases a chemical called oxytocin, also known as the love or cuddle hormone. And because of this hormone, you view your partner as more desirable than anyone else in the world. So, let me rephrase that your partner is staring at you because they're in love with you. That's one of the psychological facts about love."

He was not much interested in chemistry but highly interested in the phenomenon. She continued…….

Predictability

"According to a study in the Journal 'Human Brain Mapping', brain scans show whether or not your love is going to last. How did they come to this conclusion? Researchers scanned the brains of people in the early stages of a relationship. When the results were examined, every brain scan showed signs of love, but only a few scans showed activity in the reward and motivation centers of the brain. It turns out that the group was far more likely to stay on with their partners. Now, these same researchers checked in with their participants 18 months later and found most of these couples were still happily in love."

Why was this Professor citing this research in an otherwise exciting topic sort of annoyed the Officer? However, Dr. Spike knew just too well how to cover all the aspects of love, so she continued …..

Instinctive Protection

"Falling in love means fully accepting vulnerability. However, it's not always natural or easy for many people. Why? This is because love has an adverse reaction where instead of encouraging them to open up, they become guarded and distant. This is especially problematic for men who struggle with commitment. They're often scared to express themselves or put their emotions on the line. So, once they do fall in love, they sort of feel trapped and tend to pull away. Luckily, patience and good communication can prevent such thoughts."

Hahaha…..yes, yes….he remembered that it took long for him to open up that way. He confessed to Dr. Iyenger once that he was too shy. Dr. Spike continued…..

Attention

"Why do you want to know every little thing about your partner or the person you fancy or the one you love? Normally, we only pay attention to the big stuff like life changes, crises, success stories. I mean, even with friends and family, we rarely pay attention to the tiny details of their life. However, when love comes into the scene, it changes the way we pay attention physically and emotionally. As soon as we fall in love, the smallest details, we notice. Minuscule changes in a partner's appearance, we notice. We begin to notice even the minor quirks and habits. Love makes us care about the details of their day, the people they talk to, and even the food they ate."

So very true. Officer recalled he had undergone all those emotions. Dr. Spike continued….

Oral Categorization

"As soon as your partner makes plans, do they say I or we? After falling in love, our language begins to change without realizing it. We stop referring to ourselves and start referring to 'our' relationship as a single unit. Okay, let me make that clear. So, rather than saying I'm going to a holiday party this weekend, you may instinctively say we're going to a holiday party this weekend. This change in language tells you two things; you're happy in your relationship, and you're in it for the long term."

He remembered often telling Dr. Iyenger, we shall always be one. Of course, she would often say that too.

By now, neither had realized that the cruise had ended, and they had just talked and talked. As they walked down the gangway, they also realized they had not even eaten the free dinner as both were deeply engrossed in conversation, even though it was one-sided. She loved explaining, and he loved to listen. However, both were now hungry. Someone suggested that a Lebanese Stall that sold kababs was open till late at night, only ten minutes by walk. So they walked there and ordered Kababs. While they ate, she sat next to him and caressed the back of his neck at times. He loved that feeling, and she did that more than once. They both decided to walk back to their hotel when dinner was over, about two kilometers from there. He put his hand around her waist as they walked, and she was pleased to have it there.

After they reached the outside of her room in the hotel, she gave him the cutest smile ever. He felt it was a passionate cue, so he raised his head to kiss her on her lips. However, Dr. Spike was not interested in any such passionate encounter with the Officer but instead told him that she would meet him in the lobby again the next day, post-lunch.

There she was after her work session. He greeted her with a warm, affectionate hug and kiss on her cheek. Then, they decided to stroll back to the bank of river Danube. Her smile had some sort of a captivating appeal. He indeed had an urge to kiss those luscious lips but was afraid of losing her friendship and the remarkable bond they had established.

Officer thought SFO would have probably given it a try in his unique way. As per SFO's thinking, the ultimate expression of getting close to a woman was to sleep with her in intimacy for any well-bred man. The Officer never subscribed to that idea, and that was always a moot point between them. However, since the Officer respected SFO a lot, he would never argue but only smile when SFO lectured him. He wondered whether SFO would ever understand real romance or taking romance forward one step at a time. No way, he thought. Instead, SFO would shout and say, "What Fuckin real or fake romance? Romance is romance!"

SFO had taken retirement from the Navy as he wanted to give back to the community he grew up in by teaching poor kids, doing social work, etc. Even then, the bond between the Officer and SFO had developed from strength to strength. When the Officer called to update SFO of his talk with Dr. Spike the previous night, he told him, "While you clear your mind, make sure you enjoy her company and see to it that she has a good impression of Indians in case you get to take things to the next level." Behind every light-hearted comment of SFO, there was an underlying message to take every moment seriously. The Officer told him, "Sir, I shall make sure that I can gain something from this highly virtuous woman, considering her desire to help me."

As he continued to reflect over the conversation he had with SFO the previous night, Dr. Spike asked Officer, "What are you thinking about? How lucky would that person be who got to kiss me?" He was thinking that but was afraid to acknowledge it. So instead, he joined in her big loud laughter, and she gave him a friendly peck on his shoulder and said, "Remember, no one is as lucky enough to get a one-to-one lesson from me like you got yesterday."

"You know when I speak, people pay to listen," she said. "Then why did you think that I was the right candidate for your lecture? Although, I loved all those coherent aspects of love that you taught me." By then, they reached the bench area on the bank of Danube. She rested her head on his shoulder and gestured that he stays quiet. He did not attempt to kiss her, even though knowing that SFO would blast him for not trying hard enough.

About half an hour had passed, and the Officer was thoroughly enjoying Professor's head on his shoulder. There was something so subtle that he was finding so familiar. Ooookkkk. He realized that it was the fragrance of the same lavender perfume that Dr. Iyenger used to wear. That scent with the skin's natural fragrance was driving him mad. As he continued to be in his dreamy state, Dr.Spike unexpectedly asked him, "You told me that your girlfriend was pure vegetarian, and you a hardcore nonvegetarian. How did you manage?" Officer was literally startled by Dr. Spike's question. He laughed aloud and said, "You are a Professor, so you should tell me."

Dr. Spike smiled and said

Compromise

"In any healthy relationship where there is love, compromise is the bedrock. However, did you know that love makes it easier to compromise? You see, the more love-struck you are, the more willing you are to compromise with your partner. This is because when you love someone, you care about their needs as much as your own. You want them to feel satisfied and supported even if you have to give something up. On the other hand, if you're in a relationship but not in love, you're less willing to compromise your needs. Instead, you'll care about yourself more than your partner. Put differently. You're more likely to be stubborn and tormented by most of the decisions made by your spouse when you're not in love with them."

She was so right, he thought. She continued…

Gratitude

"Partners who are in love always want to make each other happy. They enjoy doing favors and making small sacrifices. However, love thrives off of gratitude. So, if you do your partner a favor, but they don't appreciate you, your feelings of love can backfire. Coupled with that, the disappointment will discourage you from doing your partner favors in the future. This could adversely affect the love over time. But if your partner does appreciate your contributions, their gratitude rewards and recognizes your love shall always be satisfying. As a result, this will keep your partnership strong and healthy."

"So in lecture mode again? " asked the Officer. The Professor laughed and said, "Of course! I never said I had finished. And, you know a person is happiest when they do what they love to do, so you stay quiet and listen, and yes, don't take your shoulder away. My head needs rest. So be attentive and listen like a good baby ."

She continued with a subtle laugh.

Love and Physical health

"According to Harvard health publishing, long-term relationships may increase the lifespan of the average male. What they mean here is that men in long-term relationships not only live longer, they're also happier on average. These committed men are more satisfied, less anxious, and physically healthier than single men. Now, love doesn't guarantee every man a long and healthy life; however, the results speak for themselves."

She continued

Coming to Terms with Opposition

"A lot of people wonder whether partners should be similar or different. Well, the answer is a little bit of both. Why? Because relationships are stronger when partners have similar interests and values. However, that doesn't mean you and your partner should be the same. Personality differences, for instance, enhances the likelihood of long-term love. Just think about relationships like a puzzle to make it easy for you to understand what I'm saying. Now, if you have two of the same puzzle pieces, we both know they aren't going to fit together. Why? Because you only need one of each puzzle piece to do a puzzle. This is why a loving relationship contains two different puzzle pieces which complement each other's strengths. So, if you found the right person, your opposite edges will fit together perfectly, and that is the way love operates."

Rhythm

"Love is directly linked to music. Do your favorite songs make you think of your crush? Yes, that is what I'm talking about. When you're in love, you naturally associate music with the person you love. Why? Because music is a natural source of passion, emotion, and energy. Thus, if you're in love, your brain associates all of those things with your partner or your crush. So, don't be surprised if every known song reminds you of love. It was meant to be that way. "

Never before in his life was an Officer so intrigued on this subject. While he remained spellbound, the Professor spoke for hours. Was it her delivery and knowledge on the characteristics central to love, or did he find any trace of Dr. Iyenger in her? He again smiled to himself as he knew that SFO would ask him only one question late at night. As he was thinking about that, he let out a controlled laugh. "What's so funny," asked Dr. Spike. He unsuccessfully hid his sheepish smile as he did not reply but gestured with his hand, indicating nothing. She held his neck with her big palm and lovingly shook it and laughed, saying. "I know there is something, but it's okay. I won't push you for an answer."

It was a beautiful evening, with time has flown by. The day after tomorrow, both were scheduled to leave for their respective destinations. Officer was booked for Vienna, and the Professor was booked to go to Venice. She had been to Venice many times over. However, she believed that city was losing its charm. As for the Officer, he was travelling to this side of Europe for the first time and was amazed at the beauty of the place, people, and divine nature. Every female he saw felt she was right out of the cover pages of Cosmopolitan or Vogue.

"I have an idea!" exclaimed the Professor. "Let's go to Prague. It is a beautiful place." "Capital of Czech Republic," asked the Officer. "Yes!" replied the Professor. She told the Officer that her travel desk would do the needful to arrange their travel and stay. Officer was super excited. He was to travel with the lady who he found so charismatic. And, then there were additional chances of achieving something that SFO would love to know about.

On her instructions, the travel desk arranged a road trip. Both were picked up by the limousine driver from the lobby of the hotel. Officer was impressed to notice the driver's politeness, even though his English was not that good. However, the Professor knew many languages and was conversing with the driver in German. The driver, who seemed to be a middle-aged man, was of Turkish descent and now settled in Germany working for this large travel company.

That was the best road journey of about six hours the Officer had undertaken. The driver was telling about areas through which they drove. The lush greenery appeared so familiar to the Officer. The grasslands were enchanting, blooming wildflowers, but most of all, the landscape of small red flowers of the poppy plant took his breath away. Throughout the journey, Professor caressed his extended forearm glancing at him lovingly at times. He simply adored that beautiful feeling.

Along the way, they passed through Brno, a beautiful city that seemed so crowded now. The driver spoke about this city's 'Cafe culture' and drove to the famous 'Kutna Hora.' St Barbara's Cathedral was so breathtaking. Officer did not want this journey to finish. Fields of blue lavender flowers almost left him hypnotized. Officer requested the driver to stop on the side of the road for a few minutes. He wanted to breathe in all that fragrant air that Dr. Iyenger used to emanate that seemed to now come from this mysterious Professor. He was transfixed in a delighted state of mind.

Finally, they reached Prague and checked into their respective rooms. The Professor had already told him that she loved her space and they would have separate rooms. Officer had acknowledged that but was more confused and unable to define his developing likeness for the Professor.

As a habit, Officer would share the days happening with SFO every evening. SFO scolded him and said in clear words, "If you don't express your desire or inner feelings, and maybe even make love to her, you will never be able to get close to her." "But Sir, you know very well that I just cannot do that. After Dr. Iyenger, the only person I have made love to is my wife". He continued, "Even though more often than not, making love to her is more with a sense of duty and not intense enjoyment, which should be the case. The reason being, whenever I get to that state, Dr. Iyenger comes in front of my eyes. I feel that she is looking at me." SFO retorted, "Oh my god, idiots will remain idiots, howsoever hard I work to brainwash them." "Listen to me, my son, you need to move on. You cannot stop living just because someone who died so many years ago took away your enthusiasm with them" Officer could not imagine SFO being disheartened at his inability to come out of his mental block and fixation for Dr. Iyengar.

He realized that SFO was doing the best he could in his wisdom just to ensure that Officer finds peace and moved on with his life.

Prague: 2005

A devastatingly beautiful city, the capital of the Czech Republic. It seemed as though there were more tourists in the town than locals. Officer had never seen such charming people ever before. He could feel a breath of fresh air touching deep down his lungs. Even the water from the tap was so delicious that the Officer felt like continuously drinking it. It was a taste he had never experienced before.

As they stepped out of the hotel, Dr. Spike and he strolled through typical narrow European cobbled streets in the old town. They picked up a sandwich each and a cup of coffee as they sat on the side of the old town square (Staromestske Namesti). There was always a big crowd in the area to see the fascinating Prague Astronomical Clock, with a couple of beautiful churches around.

How most of the couples sitting there were looking so lovingly in their partner's eyes? How could they stare so intently into each other's eyes? The Officer loved to watch people and wonder what was going on in their minds. That was his hobby. When he spoke of the thoughts in his mind, Dr. Spike laughed so aloud that the coffee almost spilled out of her mouth. She adored the innocent and casual comments the Officer made from time to time. She loved the simplicity and naivety of Military Officers as a genre.

She explained.

Joint Heartbeat

"According to one study from the University of California, Davis, couples connect on a unique physical level. Researchers found that heartbeats will synchronize when partners stare into each other's eyes. When loving partners develop such a strong bond, their hearts actually beat together."

That was a great revelation for the Officer. Professor continued.

Love is never lost

"Divorce is one of the scariest things in any marriage. Why? Because just when you thought you found your soul mate, who you would have wanted to spend your life with, things start to fall apart. Eventually, it disappears altogether. But here is the thing about love. When love is lost, love is found. So, that doesn't mean that you'll never love again. Putting it in perspective, a small percentage of people find lifelong happiness in their first marriage. And, around forty percent of first marriages end in divorce or separation in western society, but most people marry again. Thus, if you've experienced a divorce, remember that divorce isn't the end of your love life. Sooner or later, you will find someone you love even more. I must say in this regard, I find your or rather the eastern civilisation's value system remarkable. Ninety percent of marriages last till the death of a partner. Even if there is a loveless marriage, it invariably lasts. The main reason is family and societal bonding and stigma attached to divorce, irrespective of a reason. However, that doesn't stop partners from loving another person outside of marriage, even without knowing the person they are in love with, too closely or physically. I shall explain to you that phenomenon at an appropriate time." And she moved her long fingers in the Officer's hair with tenderness in a show of friendly affection.

However, this action made the Officer get more confused. He felt bewildered as he could not fathom the depth of Professor's wisdom, but most of all, her inner feelings. However, she was unequivocal in her stated expressions, which amazed the Officer how she could make so many statements so confidently.

Now listen to this also, and she continued.

Love's Illumination

"According to one study, love can change your entire outlook on the world. How was this conclusion made? The study tested 245 young adults over nine months. They discovered that individuals in love were significantly more optimistic than people who weren't. In other words, the presence of a partner can change the way you think and make the world a brighter place, not only for the others around you. All it takes is for you to find love. But, it is also about proper timing, you know." she continued. "Let me talk about Soul Mates," she said.

Soul Mates

"Timing and space too. One intriguing psychological fact about love is that you never know when or where you'll fall in love. You may fall for a close friend, you may develop feelings for someone at work, or maybe you'll find love in the skies or during travel. In fact, according to a survey of 50,000 travelers, 1 in 50 people met someone they love during their travel. So, the next time you're on a plane, talk to the people sitting next to you. You never know who you might meet and fall in love with."

Officer laughed aloud. "In my country, most marriages are still arranged, predominantly by parents." This time Professor laughed aloud and said, "I know that. It was falling in love I was talking about, not marriage per se. Why do you culminate every human relation into marriage?" She said with a smile while she also winked her left eye. "Someday, you will understand what/who are soulmates, the phenomenon, instant attraction, etc.."

The coffee and sandwich were long over. She was possibly fatigued talking to him for so long. "Put your head in my lap.". Although a little perplexed, he listened to her and did it rather willingly. He then felt her lips on his forehead. She kissed his eyes and said, "There is a lot I wish to tell you so that you come out of the melancholy you are experiencing for the last so many years." Officer was touched by her concern but failed to comprehend why she was doing that. "I am so confused, I surely loved Dr. Iyenger. I do not even know how to define my feelings for you. I know this is definitely not infatuation. Then what is it? Why do I feel that Dr. Iyenger is looking at me and teasing me when I am with you? Can you please elaborate more on the infatuation phenomenon? You explain things with such simplicity and a natural flow that I love listening to you, as it gives me so much solace." She kissed his forehead with all her tenderness again. He felt close to her and thought, how can lips connect one into the inner depths of someone through the forehead? Dr. Spike broke his thoughts as she spoke again.

How to tell if you're in love or just infatuation

"So, are you infatuated, or are you in love? Or are you at least on your way to being in love? I shall explain how to ascertain whether you're just infatuated or you're in love. Plus, what the warning signs are, which shows that infatuation is taking over you. Now, why is this important? Well, as I said earlier, infatuation can and does lead to some very unhealthy relationships. So, you want to make sure that you are a little over infatuated, that you are aware of it, and hopefully transition it into real love. With that in mind, let's proceed to discuss the ways."

Now listen to some chemistry.

Neurotransmitters

"First things first, infatuation is dopamine and testosterone-fueled. Put differently, and these pleasurable and rush-filled hormones are why you often have that feeling of over-excitement when you meet someone you just suddenly fell in love with. On the other hand, love is oxytocin and vasopressin fueled. Now, you're not going to know which neurotransmitters are causing your feelings, but you can know what the symptoms of each are. Vasopressin and oxytocin relate to love to give you that warm, connected, glowing kind of love. They make you feel close to that person, feel safe and connected to them. Dopamine is more likely to give you that fix. It's more likely to make you want to jump them instantly, make you feel high every time you're around them. It makes you poise towards wanting them and spending more time with them, making them feel very addictive. Now, you can have both operating at the same time, but the more you're operating under the influences of oxytocin and vasopressin, the more likely you're on the love spectrum rather than the infatuation spectrum. In other words, it's either you're in love or infatuated. The two can't coexist as one will have to give way to the other over time."

Officer requested her not to stop, and she carried on.

Longevity

"This is another point that I stated at the early phase of our talk. The reality is that love takes a lot more time, and infatuation is more like instantaneously. If it's only been two dates and you can't stop thinking about them, again, that's likely to be the dopamine fix of infatuation, telling you to think, think, think about them every waking moment. Love takes longer to develop, which means you're not going to have the same obsessive thought patterns with infatuation. This is another reason why love conquers all."

Physical Attraction

"I guess I should have brought this as the first point number because quite frankly, most infatuation is often stimulated from the physical attributes of a person. Infatuation is very physical. By physical, I don't necessarily mean that you're obsessed with how they look and their physical appearance, though that may be the case. Nevertheless, infatuation can often come from what it can do to your physical body. The way they look at you, the way they smile at you, what it does to your body. Infatuation is very, very physical, whereas love is deeper and more emotional. Love sees beyond the physical and goes deeper into creating a soul bond. This is why love remains even when physical attributes of a person fade away."

"What is this soul bond," asked the Officer. Dr. Spike was all smiles and promised to explain to him, but first, she wanted to talk about something else. So she continued,

Quality Profoundness

"So this is a big one that I talk to people in India about. It is pretty easy to know when someone is driven by infatuation rather than love. How do I know this easily? By asking them questions. First, I'll ask you what you like about the person and what you do not like. From here on, their response will tell you all you need to know. Most times, their list tends to be infatuation-based traits, superficial things, etc. For instance, you'll start hearing things like it's the way she looks at me. It's her smile. It's how much fun she is. It's how genuine she seems. It's *how cool she is,* and all this is over just a short period. Whereas, when they say these are the things that I don't like about him, he's a poor communicator, dishonest, doesn't put in a lot of effort, etc., are natural traits that you never let you fall in love with that person.

Infatuation is about much more superficial things and, again, what these things do to you. Whereas love is about much deeper traits and hence it takes time to come out of it."

Blind Eyes to Bad Attributes

"Infatuation doesn't see any negative traits. Everything is good. Oh, she's messy, but it's okay; I love her that way. I'm 'OCD' clean, so we balance each other out nicely. Infatuation cannot see any negatives, or even if it does, it manages to turn them all into positives. Love, on the other hand, sees the negatives but loves despite these negatives. Love doesn't play a blind face when things are not going right, as it always finds a way to work things out. Overall, infatuation feelings are fake and unrealistic, while love is real and not sugar-coated."

Spirit of Oneness

"The spirit of oneness is one that I can personally vouch for. It still feels like 'you' and 'him/her' as independent entities when you're infatuated. However, when you're in love, there's a sense of unity. When you think about that person, it's we, not me and him anymore but us! Like I said earlier, love creates a soul bond that will enable the two of you to connect deeply, thus become one."

Unpredictability

"Infatuation is always unpredictable. You never know whether you're going to get ghosted. What's going to happen next? Where is this going? Love is more predictable. Infatuation can disappear on a whim. But, on the other hand, love has a path, and as such, it's highly predictable."

Fake Lifestyle

"One of the tell-tale signs of infatuation is you start doing a whole bunch of different things that you would never do, just to appease or please your partner. You find yourself doing things, hanging out with people, taking up things that you never would've done before. Now it's not to say that you shouldn't be open-minded. However, it is not something that could be stemming from within. On the other hand, love can be open-minded, and love can certainly explore new areas to grow as an individual by opening up and opening yourself up to your partner's interests. So, love will make you do things because you want to. Love will do it because it genuinely wants to grow and have experience in that area. You will also have no problem saying, *Nah, I tried it. I don't like it, so back to what I do*. Infatuation, on the other hand, will cause us to be obsessed. We'll tolerate doing things, saying things, and be a person that you wouldn't usually be. It makes you become a stranger to yourself."

Oh my god, exclaimed Officer, "It's already 1930 hrs, and I have not asked you even for a glass of water. How unofficer like! That was one thing no officer can digest; being unchivalrous. He offered to fetch locally brewed wine for her from a bistro a few meters across, and she smiled in agreement. She had taken a challenge onto herself that she would bring the Officer out of his latent sadness inflicted on him by that eventful air crash. She knew that few incidents leave a strong impression on your mind and require more than normal efforts to reverse their effects.

He came back with wine and two glasses. At the back of his mind, he also knew, both he and the Professor were to leave Prague after two days, and there was only a concise time for him to imbibe more and more.

He was at his charming best when he almost pleaded to Dr. Spike to tell him more, as he felt she might be feeling drained talking almost non-stop. But, lucky for him, she continued.

Aftermath Emotions

"Infatuation leads to subsequent negative emotions, whereas love leads to subsequent positive emotions. Okay, so what do I mean by this? While infatuation is at a high, it becomes unsustainable. Inevitably that high has to come down to a low point. Then, you'll start comparing the point where you are, to the point where you were, thus, and feel negative about it. It raises those expectations so high that you can't possibly feel good in comparison. Love, on the other hand, pushes you to source your positive emotions from yourself. It pushes you to grow, and it pushes you to change and expand yourself as a person. So when you're in love, you start feeling better and better as a result. In a nutshell, infatuation leads to a crash, whereas love pushes you up in the air."

Forced conversations

"Infatuation can't have tough conversations because it avoids them at all cost. Everyone wants to pretend and play fair even when their feelings have been hurt. Love, on the other hand, deals with them and gets through the problem. Infatuation is perfect, right? It feels perfect. It feels great. So the last thing you want to do is ruin that dynamic by having a difficult conversation or blowing the fantasy. It's tough to have difficult conversations with someone you're infatuated with and get through them. You just don't want to ruin that perfect dynamic. That's how infatuation feels. At the same time, Love can have those conversations because love knows that it will survive those conversations. There is no pretending which still goes to prove the point that love is as real as it gets."

Foundation

"Infatuation is almost often based on projections; projections of who they are as a person. Projections on what your relationship will be. Infatuation has to be based on projections because there's not enough information for it to be accurate. Love, on the other hand, is based on what you have seen. It's based on the experiences you have had and the memories that were real. Put differently, infatuation is based on projections, whereas love is based on real-life experiences.

Having said this, you should be able to tell if you have an infatuation or it's true love you're feeling. However, it doesn't just end here. If you're infatuated, then you need to get over yourself, stop pranking yourself and go for something real; go for love. Love is a beautiful thing, except that many myths are often circulated about it, making it confusing for some people to understand fully."

The Officer told her about the severe shock he got when he learned that Dr. Iyenger was married. He felt much more devastated with that than the news of her death. He could not stop wondering, why did she conceal such a significant fact from him? Why Swami Iyer had to take him to their house for him to learn this fact at a time when she was no more? The questions were haunting me ever since that day. Dr. Spike was stunned too. Her researches and experience could not answer his questions instantly. The Officer thought it was unfair to push her to give him answers after a whole afternoon of non-stop talk.

It was late evening by now. Just a few meters across the park was the Prague State Opera, built-in 1888. A beautiful historic place. Chicago Philharmonic Orchestra was to play there that evening, and the Officer managed to get two tickets. He thought it was the least he could do for Dr. Spike. While seated and waiting for the concert to begin, he told Dr. Spike about his closeness with SFO. He had a picture of him on his phone that he showed to Dr. Spike. He told her that he planned to show him her picture as well. He praised SFO as being a really good and genuine soul, always concerned about the well-being of others. Dr. Spike was happy to know about SFO.

Out of all the performances that evening, the Officer loved Beethoven's ninth symphony. It was one of his favourite compositions, and whenever he got a chance, he would not miss hearing that. Doctor Spike was amazed at his passion and knowledge of western classical music. She, too, was fond of music. After the concert, they went straight back to the hotel. For the Officer and possibly for Dr. Spike, it was indeed a memorable day of sorts.

Vaclav Havel (Prague) airport was around one hour from their hotel. He insisted on seeing her off at the airport. They barely spoke during the drive. When they reached, she kissed him on his cheek and hurriedly entered the airport departure gate. The Officer returned to the hotel in the taxi. She ran to the washroom as she did not want anyone to see her crying. Her tears just would not stop. How much she had wished that the Officer made love to her. For the first time, perhaps she restrained herself from making love to someone when she really wanted it. That was because she had taken the Officer as one of her subjects whom she was trying to help get out of a situation that had plagued their mind. But then, she had gotten deeply attracted to him during those few days. She knew that such an attachment phenomenon was not rare. The therapist and subject do get deeply attached. But, she was a seasoned Professor who was super ethical towards her profession.

Finally, her flight took off, and the aircraft banked on the starboard side, and both of them were only left with memories of the past few days.

IV
Astrology and Karmik connection of Souls

"Our souls already know each other. Don't they ?."
'It is our bodies that are new.'
Karen Ross

2008 Vaidheeshwaran (Tamil Nadu) and Hoshiarpur (Punjab)

Swami Iyer and the Officer had developed a great bond of respect and friendship. Officer used to love to listen to Iyer, and the latter was too happy to oblige. But, deeply emotional as he was, Swamy Iyer was disturbed at the constant melancholy that had set in the Officer's mind, who wanted to know why Dr. Iyenger had hidden such an important fact of her marriage from him. But, on the other hand, the Officer was convinced that Dr. Iyenger deeply loved him. So he felt deeply loved yet sad at the same time.

One day Swami Iyer asked the Officer whether he knew the date of birth, time, and place of Dr. Iyenger. Officer replied in affirmative. Iyer told the Officer that a friend of his was pursuing astrological studies at the largest school of astrology in the world at Delhi, namely 'Bhartiya Vidya Bhavan' (BVB) under the patronage of much-revered astrologer Mr. KN Rao. Mr. Rao had been credited with getting super spiritual science 'Astrology' from secretive annals of traditional pandits. Mr. Rao also had a highly competent faculty consisting of

Engineers, lawyers, Civil Servants, Scientists, etc. All of whom were highly competent astrologers to assist him in educating people who joined his institute. As per Iyer, his friend was a student of Mr. Manoj Pathak, a much-respected teacher, and was doing important research as part of his astrology class course. This friend had asked Iyer to get Dr. Iyenger's birth details for analysis.

On giving the birth details of Dr. Iyengar to Iyer's friend, the Officer was constantly questioning Iyer as to how astrology came into being, how charts were written, etc. Seeing the officer's sudden interest in astrology-related aspects, Iyer decided to take the Officer to Vaidheeshwaran in Tamil Nadu. The place was famous for an ancient temple where unmarried girls prayed to get good and competent husbands. They also prayed and for help for obviating delays in their marriage. However, the fascinating thing about the place was that it was also considered the seat of Nadi astrology.

Some background

Officer knew about the subject only to the extent that an individual's horoscope can throw some light on events in an individual's life. However, as they were headed there, Swami Iyer thought it was best to educate the Officer a little more, so he started,

"Astrology is not only the art of Fortune/ future predicting, but it is a divine science that comes from our ancient scriptures."

"Jyotish means "Light of God." It is a branch of Vedanga (Veda) so Vedanga is part of Vedas."

Officer, as usual, was listening to Iyer with rapt attention as Iyer continued.

"Astrology tells us about our purpose of life by placing planets in the horoscope, varga charts, various dashas that are the timing of events. There are very many dashas described in scriptures. Commonly used dashas are Vimshotri, Yogini, Jaimini, Parashari, etc., etc., Then there are various techniques, viz Naadi, Bhrigu, Varshphal, KP, etc. emanated or are part of Vedic astrology. "

"Astrology as a science has been developed to study the influence of planets and nakshatras (stars) on human beings. To be an astrologer, one has to have reasonable knowledge of mathematics to understand the concept of the movement of planets and have a mind that can analyze and synthesize. There can be numerous combinations of houses, planets, signs, nakshatras, etc., and no computer can do justice. As of this date, it is the only human mind that can do the kind of synthesis required to achieve results with reasonable accuracy. The limitation is not in science but the human mind limited by its ability to decipher due to its complexities. As more and more researches are being carried out all over the world, especially at BVB Delhi, more and more facts are coming out regularly."

"Astrology is a divine science and as enormous as all oceans put together. Therefore, one requires unique abilities to learn even the basics. Those basics are explained in the first chapter of 'Brhad Prashar Hora

Shastra, the ultimate scripture on the subject authored by Rishi Parashar."

"Astrology is a super science where every principle can be modeled as in science, subjected to scientific analysis, experimented with acceptable samples, with reliable and verifiable results with 100% percent validity." Swami Iyer further explained, "Astrology is not just only predicting the future, but it can provide us guidance to cut down the bad Karma and follow the path of Moksha."

Nadi Astrology

Officer was intrigued more and more as they reached Vaidheeshwaran Koel. Koel, in the local language, meant temple. And what a great temple it was. Officer felt energetic vibrations as he entered. The fragrance of smoke from essence sticks and other worship material had engulfed the whole surrounding area. There was a long queue of young girls praying to get good husbands! Priests wearing only dhoti and nothing on top were moving to and fro in the area reserved for them, showing sacred fire to worshippers for obeisance and asking for Dakshina (charity). The whole place was saturated with spiritual richness. Officer felt his eyes fill up with the emotion of a different kind, as he felt some sort of release. He profusely missed Dr. Iyenger.

Officer and Swami Iyer came out and saw a writing 'Nadi Astrology' on a giant board outside one tiny shop. Officer realized that every second shop in that area was displaying similar boards. They entered one of them randomly. The boy at the counter seated them and wherein Swami signaled to the boy to take a thumb impression of the Officer. Swami Iyer did not give him, as he had done that many times before.

Officer learned that Nadi astrologers were brilliant and could narrate our past, present, and future, up to the level of one's spiritual journey till Moksha. They did that by taking a thumb impression, and on that basis, they would locate pre-written texts on 'Palm leaves.' The writings were in the local language, and being written on those sheets meant that the scripts are available for a long time. Surprisingly for every thumb impression, they would identify one palm leaf and retrieve it amongst numerous bundles. With a small error and elimination exercise, they would generally get the exact one written for a particular person. Just to see them going up and down several of the leaves were indeed unique and overwhelming. Officer was stunned when a Tamil scholar finally picked out his Palm leaf. He was further shocked when the scholar started by telling him the names of his father, mother, the place he belonged to, and so many personal details known only to the Officer. Surprises are the best fodder for the mind, and the Officer was indeed spellbound listening to what the scholar was reading. The assistant to Tamil scholar recorded the whole narration of the present, past, and future regarding Officer meticulously on an audio cassette. The Officer's jaw fell open with the accuracy of the narration of his history and present ongoing events. There was no way to validate the future, but even the future was very likely to be very accurate if one went by trend, thought the Officer.

Officer was clearly and categorically told that he would fall in love with a lady in a medical profession who would not live long. As the scholar read this from one of the leaves, it was as if the universe stared in the Officer's face. He was stunned. He was speechless. His jaw remained open in awe. Officer then requested the Tamil scholar to tell him more about 'astrology' as such. However, the scholar said he was duty-bound elsewhere but would be glad to see them in the evening. Swami Iyer told the scholar of the restaurant nearby where they could meet in the evening after his work for the day was over. The Officer gave the scholar heavy Dakshina (charity) in addition to his fees.

When they met at the restaurant, Iyer ordered some south Indian snacks and coffee. The scholar began to educate the Officer on astrology. He said,

"All branches of astrology are based on Karma theory. It is the total of our past birth's Karmas, and depending on our cumulative Karmas of previous lives, we get a good or bad planetary position in the present birth. The Jyotish is further divided into three parts – Ganit, Samhita, and Hora."

"Ancient scholars chose to work with nine planets and 27 Nakshatra in astrology. With the help of various astrological tools like the Dasha, transit, prashna, and natal promise, we can get insight into any event of life, good or bad."

Officer was learning something entirely new.

"Status of the profession, quality of marriage, mode of education, health-related issue, love relationship, etc. all these are indicated in our horoscope. One has to be an astute astrologer to answer any question as this science is very tough and should not be used only for fortune-telling. Its ultimate purpose is to enhance the spiritual growth of the native."

"Generally horoscope of family members, friends and loved ones for that matter are interconnected or similar because their destiny and good or bad events are linked."

Officer and Swami Iyer listened with rapt attention as they sipped the hot filtered coffee. Officer loved the flavor of that freshly brewed coffee, but it was not his focus. The Tamil scholar continued,

Karma and Astrology

"We get our horoscope based on per our past Karma, if one did good Karma, they would get good planets in the Kundali (horoscope) with positives in their life, while if one did bad Karma in the past, they would get an afflicted horoscope with more negatives in their life."

"In some classical texts, we get some hint about past life connections. For example, Dr. Brian Weiss, in his books, has recorded cases of past life connection.."

Tamil scholar quoted from Bhagwad Geeta,

"अवश्यमेव भोक्तव्यं कृतं कर्म शुभाऽशुभम्।

नाभुक्तं क्षीयते कर्म कल्प कोटि शतेरऽपि॥"

Meaning- One has to suffer for his karmas. The result of any action done, either good or bad, has to be experienced. It can't be forfeited even after thousands of years.

केवलं ग्रह नक्षत्रं न करोति शुभाशुभं ।

सर्वमात्रकृतं कर्मं लोकवादो ग्रहा इति ॥

Meaning- it's not only planets and stars which give auspicious and inauspicious results. But it is all the result of one's karmas through belief."

Officer was truly intrigued. He asked a very relevant question from the scholar,

"What is Karma and what is not Karma ?"

Scholar replied

Karma and Free Will

"It's not at all complicated to understand what karma is? Whatever we are doing is all Karma. If our actions make others happy, it becomes Satkarma (good deeds), and if our action hurts others and gives them pain, it's Dushkarma (bad deeds). It also includes our daily routine activities like Nitya karma, for example, bathing, etc. We cannot live without Karma. "

"If a person has done all negative Karma in a previous life and not doing any sat karma in the present, they are bound to have suffering and an afflicted horoscope. God gives us a chance and free will to rectify the past Karma results. Only good Karma can reduce results of past birth's negative Karma result. Now the question may arise what is free will? Free will is the area where the person can rectify his previous negative Karma but within predestined limits and cannot go outside from it."

Officer sighed aloud and indicated to Swami Iyer to explain to him later as he did not want to stop the scholar from explaining. Swami Iyer understood and nodded his head with a wink.

Officer was thoroughly enjoying all that knowledge that was being imparted and was listening with his great intent. However, when he failed to understand some things being stated, he would wink at Iyer, and Iyer would know that he would have to explain the same to the Officer in more straightforward language.

Scholar explained further, "Astrology considered three Types of Karmas, first is 'Sanchit Karma' or accumulated (stored) Karma of all previous births. It cannot be changed. These are responsible for our suffering or happiness in this birth and are analysed from the fifth house of horoscope. Then there is Prarabdh, i.e. destiny, and is decided by that portion of

Sanchit karma responsible for influencing present life. The ninth house predominantly reflects this in one's horoscope. Agami karma is a total of previous and present birth. When paap (sin) and punaya (good or pure) karma nullify each other, one attains moksha. The twelfth house of the horoscope and the positioning of Ketu in the horoscope indicate one's status of attaining moksha. Moksha is freedom from the cycle of birth and death. It is important to know that no one house gives the whole picture. It also entails the planet's position, conjunctions, aspects, and exchanges in various houses and rashis (signs)." Scholar smiled as he saw the perplexed expression on the Officer's face.

That was too much and too good information, thought the Officer. However, he felt sad as he wondered whether Dr. Iyenger attained Moksha or not. He was a great worshiper of Lord Krishna.

As scholar excused himself to go to the washroom, Swami Iyer took over,

"In Geeta, karma principles are beautifully explained. Let us discuss some." Officer did not know Sanskrit at all, but he knew Swami would explain everything. So Swami started,

" कर्मण्येवाधिकारस्ते मा फलेषु कदाचन।

मा कर्मफलहेतुर्भूर्मा ते सङ्गोऽस्त्वकर्मणि॥

81

Meaning- You have every right to work but not to expect fruits or rewards out of it. Do not focus on the fruits, nor have an attachment to inaction."

" न कर्मणामनारम्भान्नैष्कर्म्यं पुरुषोऽश्रुते।

न च संन्यसनादेव सिद्धिं समधिगच्छति॥

Meaning- No one can attain freedom from activity by refraining from action; nor can he reach perfection by merely refusing to act."

" नियतं कुरु कर्म त्वं कर्म ज्यायो ह्यकर्मण:।

शरीरयात्रापि च ते न प्रसिद्ध्येदकर्मण:॥

Meaning - Therefore, do you perform your allotted duty, for action is superior to inaction. Desisting from shifting, you cannot even maintain your body."

The scholar came back. Officer wanted to know whether it was possible to know if there was a past life connection between him and Dr. Iyenger. The scholar replied in affirmative. Officer wanted to learn more. Unfortunately, it was already midnight, and it was not right to expect the scholar to go on. The scholar told the Officer that he was going out of town the following day. However, if he was still interested, he could give him the contact details of his ex-student, who would surely answer any of his other questions to his satisfaction. Scholar told the Officer that his student was one of few experts who could also read karmic connections with great accuracy. The scholar said to the Officer, "I will write a note telling him that he should accord priority to you whenever you visit him." It was challenging to get an out-of-turn appointment with him, but the Scholar's letter would give the Officer that advantage.

The Scholar then wrote a letter on a small piece of paper adding his student's address and phone number. When the Officer looked at the address, he felt like pulling his hair. The address was Hoshiarpur, a small city in Punjab that he was so well aware of, as his own house was not too far from there. That student's name was Naveen Parashar, a north Indian Brahmin who had learned Nadi astrology at Vaidheeshwaran at the feet of the Tamil scholar.

North Indian way that was equivalent to south Indian Nadi style with pre-written text was called 'Bhrigu Padhatti.' The pre-written text is kept with many families practicing the Bhrigu technique. They all cooperate for a client and share the pre-written text best suited to a person's credentials.

Before departing, the Scholar told these two gentlemen that the techniques of both schools are the same. They were written in a similar fashion. Expertise lay in the ability to decipher the text. They understood.

Reading from Bhrigu Sanhita

Swami Iyer did not want to go to Hoshiarpur as he did not like to travel. However, the Officer was hell-bent on taking him along as he felt very comfortable in the company of Swami Iyer. After much deliberation, they decided to visit Hoshiarpur after three months. Swami Iyer thought the visit would undoubtedly provide an excellent opportunity to enhance his knowledge. They spoke to Pandit Naveen Parashar and fixed an appointment accordingly.

When they met Pandit Parashar, he greeted them with great respect as his teacher had referred them to him. Officer right away told him that he wished to know about his past life connects with Dr. Iyenger. While Iyer had some astrology training, he did not know complex aspects and the highly advanced Nadi techniques associated with karmic connections.

Before Pandit Naveen could even start speaking, both of them requested that he give them more than his usual time so that the Officer could clarify all kinds of questions bothering him and sort of stressed him out. Pandit agreed. The Officer was relieved and happy.

Pandit began informally chatting with Officer and Iyer about horoscopes and planets, in general.

Shri Ram and Ravan

"Lord Ram and Ravan both had good horoscopes. They had many exalted good planets, but Ravan's bad karmas ensured that Lord Rama defeated him. Ravan did not listen to his elders; hence his Sun becomes malefic. He ditched out younger brother 'Vibhishan' so his Mars got afflicted. He kidnapped another's wife and did not respect his own wife, so his Venus got affected. He converted the positive strength of the exalted planets into negative by attracting paap (sin) karma.

On the other hand, Lord Rama followed his father's words, obeyed his mother, took care of his brother Lakshman and fought for his wife. As a result, he had a great win over Ravan as lord Ram made his planets more potent by attracting punya (good) karmas. So we can easily say that all astrology depends on the Karma factor." "Wow," exclaimed the two.

Pandit often got a good audience, but then there was something special in these two. He could see their eyes were radiating as they spoke while their expressions seemed as though they were astonished at the information just given. He then decided to share a great Nadi secret principle with them and said, "Now, I shall share with you a great Nadi principle not known to many."

A Great Secret

"It is common knowledge that Rahu and Ketu are considered planets. Although per vedic astrology, they are not physical bodies. They are shadowy mathematically arrived points formed due to the motion of the earth and moon. Simply stated, the sensitive points formed by the moon while revolving around the earth in its orbit from the Northern side of its point of intersection is 'Rahu or Dragon head' and exact 180 degrees away from this point of intersection is 'Ketu or dragon's tail.' For survival on Earth - Sun and Moon are both important planets, so their intersection points Rahu and Ketu, are crucial, impacting the lives of human beings. In many classical texts, it is written that Rahu and Ketu connect one soul to another. Hence, Rahu and Ketu are significant planets in the horoscope. Some also take the 'Jeeva' (Jupiter) in this past birth connection theory. And, that is the secret known only to a handful of good astrologers."

Swami Iyer's eyes popped up with astonishment and gleam. Officer's mouth dried up with such a wealth of information. Understanding their state, Pandit ordered lassi for all, a popular drink of Punjab made of churned curd or yogurt. The people of Punjab liked it thick and creamy and in large quantities. It came in three tall brass glasses of three fourth liter each. Swami Iyer had never seen it so rich and creamy and not so much lassi in one glass. They felt nice and cool as they took a big sip while Pandit Naveen Parashar smiled and continued,

"Sun is our soul. All new creations happen with sunlight only, and the moon is our mind, our emotion. So Rahu, Ketu, as I said before, being two points of intersection, greatly affects humankind. Rahu and Ketu are always retrograde in motion. Although the Rahu, Ketu do not have a physical body, ancient sages include them in nine planets in Vedic Hindu astrology due to their powerful influence on Earth. They give unexpected and incredible results if positively placed in the chart. "

"Now listen carefully. Here is an expansion of the above secret," the Pandit said." We all manifest our love relations, friendships, husband, wife, brother, sister, and Guru-disciple relationship by virtue of our past lives karma results. Sometimes we meet people accidentally and form a great emotional bond. It's all done by our souls due to past karmic connections with each other. We are deeply attached to some people without any formal relationship or even long associations. We feel mental agony and pain from some relationship with another set, again because of past Karma. It is like giving and taking in a relationship and continuing through the cycle of many lives and births until it can not become zero. And that is a challenge for any good astrologer to find. Deeply learned and educated ones can find out."

Pandit was happy to share his wisdom. He carried on to share an extension of the secret principle that he had mentioned.

Iyer was just too happy to learn and assimilate as much as he could. He was a great learner and would often implement his knowledge for the betterment of all around him, as that was his life mission.

Pandit Naveen further explained

Secret Continues

"How do we know the bond of a present relationship and past birth life between two souls? If the Rashi (signs) of Rahu Ketu of one person matches Rashi of Sun, moon with another person, they have possibly shared something in their past lives: travel, food, house, profession, etc. Moreover, suppose Rahu, Ketu, and Jupiter make a trinal 1,5,9 connection with the other person's Rahu, Ketu, and Jupiter. In that case, there is a strong Karmic connection between the two souls. It may have been deep love or attachment of some kind. Something like a relationship extending from one birth to another one."

It was a fantastic piece of knowledge.

Pandit Naveen continued, "People don't come accidentally in our life. They are not giving us happiness or pain by their wish. It all because of past birth debts between two souls, so let us understand with examples."

He said, "I am going to give you examples of some of the well-known personalities so that it will be easy to understand."

Nehru-Gandhi family

"If we check the horoscopes of Nehru- Gandhi family, we notice that all family members have a past birth connection. The two rules for the past birth relationship between souls apply 100% on them. From Pt J L Nehru to Varun Gandhi, Rahul Gandhi et al. have this strong connection because they all remained only in politics."

Though interested in the overall scheme of things, the Officer was not interested in anyone else's connection but only between Dr. Iyenger and himself.

He shook his head in utter disbelief when Pandit Naveen Parashar showed him all of Dr. Iyenger's and his horoscope conditions, showing the strong karmic connection and past life association. Then, Pandit read a chapter from Bhrigu records indicating how they were destined to meet again, although in a different setting. Pandit Parashar told the Officer that he would meet a lady within a few years, and the Officer's connection with that lady will be much more than just friendship. They both will just not be able to prevent a magnetic attraction between themselves. They will form a very rare, unique, and strong bond that will be difficult to decipher. It would be a bond like Radha shared with Krishna. This will happen again and again in all the births till they both attain freedom from the cycle of birth and death.

He ended by saying, "Remember what I have said." And then added, "God bless both of you."

Officer did not know what to say or how to thank him for reading a vital part of the Bhrigu record that sort of put his mind at ease. He paid hefty Dakshina to Pandit and left Hoshiarpur the same day with Swami Iyer. He was wondering why life was so mysterious and complicated. Why was he getting entangled in one mystery after another one. He felt anger and frustration but also some amount of calmness at what the Pandit had told him. He shook his head in puzzlement at how he would find her. However, he felt relieved as he thought that he was sure to meet a lady who, in her previous life/lives, would be connected to Dr. Iyenger's soul in her previous life/lives. He was stunned to learn of how advanced Indian spiritual sciences were during ancient times.

He was thinking about all this when he was distracted by a phone call from SFO telling him gossip about one sailor who pissed from balcony in a drunkard state straight on the head of local councilor much to chargin' of state police. Navy had refused to hand over that sailor to civilian authority.

SFO also excitedly told the Officer that he was delighted to secure a US visa and was soon scheduled to visit his cousin working on a farm in Fresno, a California city.

V
Love's Mystery and Society

"Mysterious love, Uncertain treasure hast thou more
of pain or pleasure !... endless torments dwell upon
thee : yet who would live and live without thee"

Joseph Addison

2007

SFO had never seen any country like this before. He was so happy in the USA. His cousin worked at Brar farms, owned by an Indian origin landlord Rashpal Singh Brar. One weekend SFO decided to visit Stanford University in Palo Alto, around 170 miles from Fresno. SFO was pretty excited as Stanford University was one of the landmarks on his bucket list that he always wanted to see in California. He had read that it was like a university town, even though Google, Facebook, Apple, and other hi-tech companies were headquartered in the area. Many visitors also thronged that area as it had some good eating places, good crowd and good shopping around it.

It was not the first time Dr. Spike had landed at San Francisco airport. She always wondered how so many people of such diverse origins worked at that airport. She was there to receive a coveted award that American Psychological Association (APA) conferred every year to the psychologist whose researches made a difference to mankind.

As Dr. Spike sipped Café Latte at one of the cafes in Stanford Mall near Standford university, she felt she saw someone familiar at the table right across from where she was seated. She had never seen that man in person but was somehow confident that she knew him well. As she continued to look at him, their eyes met, and the man on the other side almost instantly screamed her name, "Dr. Spike!" with full excitement. Dr. Spike knew that he was SFO with whom she had interacted over emails, messaging apps, etc., regarding the Officer. She was super excited. They hugged each other and were amazed at how destiny makes people meet. It was an enjoyable experience for both. Dr. Spike told SFO that she was there to attend an award ceremony at the Stanford Memorial Auditorium. It was a full day's program the following day and invited SFO to attend. SFO was too happy to accept the invite.

The next day SFO reached Stanford Memorial Auditorium thirty minutes before the scheduled time. As Dr. Spike took the stage, she saw him formally dressed, sitting in the second row as the first row was reserved for dignitaries. SFO smiled at seeing her and at his thinking of his ultimate and final goal. He recalled how he wanted the Officer to get intimate with Dr. Spike, because as per him, only then would the Officer attain peace and satisfaction. However, it was not meant to be! Nevertheless, even now, his thoughts were only focussed on those lines, and he continued to be amused with that thought.

Dr. Spike would miss the Officer so often. She used to think of his simplicity and wondered about her unique connection with him. Due to her professional work ethic, she was sure not going to get into any sort of relationship or have any intimacy with the Officer. Sometimes she would curse herself for being so prudish. Yet, she would imagine her head on his shoulders and his saintly smile. She would often email her published / in-progress work to him. Officer would read her work fondly but would always have many more unanswered questions. However, he never wanted to burden her more.

Dr Spike's Lecture at Stanford University, USA

The APA Chair invited Dr. Spike to deliver her keynote address. Her recent published researches on Mysteries of Love and Society and Contemporary Love had brought her much more fame than she already had. Every human being who had read or heard about her work identified some aspect or the other of their life with some part of her research.

The hall was filled with students, teachers, and staff from all over the University, as people would do anything to listen to her. Students were sitting on the aisle on the floor as all seats were fully occupied. Many were gladly standing.

Dr. Spike looked divine, and she commenced her talk.

Love and Mystery

"Have you ever heard someone say that love is a mystery? Well, the answer to that 'depends' isn't it? Sometimes it could be 'yes,' and other times it could be 'no.' The answer could be a 'yes' because the understanding and definition of love are not understood in its depth by anybody these days. But, when you enhance your knowledge or try and understand the boundaries of love, you'll no longer see love as a mystery at the appropriate time. It's as simple as that. Love is not a thing that waits for you to search for it every time you meet a new person. It's that eternal bliss and feeling which happens to you at some point in time in life. Don't ever wait for it to happen or try to make it happen. It's just another natural phenomenon on this earth. When it comes to you blissfully, enjoy every bit of it and live it to the fullest. Love is such a powerful thing. It can do wonders and miracles for you. It has the power to turn all the impossible to possible, including melt you, right? So, yes, love is a mystery."

"You never know when you'll fall for a person so deeply that you can't stay away from them. You will never find out why you are always thinking about your love and somehow want to see them in front of you. You'll never understand how a person who never mattered has now turned so caring and loving. You won't understand how to know what your partner must be thinking. You will never understand the logic behind experiencing the same amount of pain as your partner suffers. You'll never be able to see a single tear in their eyes. I mean, there are just uncountable examples like that. The most ironic thing about love is that you don't even know when you starting loving anyone. It is a process that is so jumbled up that isn't any procedure for anyone to fall in love!"

" However, the answer to the question of whether love is a mystery could also be a 'No.' Why? Because even though we can't solve the mystery, love only takes a spontaneous moment to occur. Put differently. It's more of a choice if you attack it during the early phase. It happens most times in life. In some cases, people stop seeing each other or date each other because of certain factors that may not complement their union. This could include things such as cultural diversity, race, and other variations in belief. Don't get me wrong. I'm not saying it isn't beautiful for an intercultural or racial union to occur. It is, and it happens often. However, this difference often prevents two people from falling in love to halt the feeling halfway in some rare scenarios. They do this not because they don't love each other but for the safety of their future. So, love is a mystery, and no, it isn't fully a mystery. However, in between these two phenomena comes the "society."

The hall was roaring with claps as she continued. Many in the gallery were shaking their heads in amazement as they were getting their answers. At one time, when clapping stopped, everybody looked at the second row. SFO was still clapping with all his energy. He clapped for almost a full minute and then stopped. Dr. Spike looked at him and gave him the cutest possible smile, and continued,

How Society Shapes the Way We Love

"More than people would love to agree. Society has influenced love now than ever. How is this possible? It starts at an early age. The way we love, our love pattern, is mostly reliant on the form of parenting experience we had as a kid. Thus, it is without a doubt that our childhood shapes us to a certain extent. This includes and is not limited to how we choose to react to different situations and the way we express ourselves, our behavioral patterns that are formed starting at a young age, and when we first begin to learn how to make sense of our immediate environment."

"This is why everyone has a certain love style based on their upbringing, And what do I mean when I say love style? I'm talking about the way people respond to their partners in a relationship. So here are the kind of love styles everyone falls into based on the effect of the society from childhood."

Universal Pleasing Lover

"These are the kind of lovers who grew up in a not so friendly, kind of home. Put differently, a home where the parents were too stringent and caging that they always tried their best not to upset them. Whenever, they got on the nerves of such parents, they would beat them to stupor. So, in that fear of not making things go wrong, such lovers grow up to become pleasers. They would do anything just to make their partners happy. Even if it means doing something unethical, they just won't care. This is the life they've known for years, and it's how they have grown comfortable to live in. While dating, ever-pleasing lovers feel terrible when things go wrong, even when it's not their fault. They take all the blame and could even run away from a relationship if it keeps happening. However, there's a solution for lovers like these. They need to get over their head and see life for what it is. They need to understand that life doesn't revolve around them, and sometimes, others are at fault."

The Victim Lover

"While growing up, these kinds of lovers always choose to conceal their thoughts and emotions inside from chaotic parents that abuse them while they are young. This causes them to build a safe haven for themselves in their head, where their thoughts flourishes. You can identify these kinds of lovers from how anxious, depressed, and unusually quiet they often get. When they are in a relationship, a victim lover will always play the victim card. They will always sabotage the partner into believing that they are always hurting them. However, for such lovers to have long-lasting and healthy relationships, they need to practice more self-love and build a voice for themselves. This will help them stand up for themselves whenever the need arises. They need to understand that the world in their head is just an illusion. This is reality."

The Manipulative Lover

"These kinds of lovers had a childhood where there was no one for them, so they had to fend and take care of themselves. They grew up strong and independent; thus, they have this illusion of always being in control. When they are in a relationship, they want what they want regardless of how the partner feels. Such lovers hate being vulnerable as it would make them appear weak. They always want to be and feel in control of everything in the relationship, and anything done without their consent is taboo. Just like every other kind of lover, there is a solution for these types. They need to understand that the world doesn't revolve around them and that it is okay for them to show their vulnerability to their partner. That way, the relationship will be healthier and less toxic."

The Hesitant Lover

"These kinds of lovers are those that grew up not knowing whether their parents loved them or not. Why? Because the love wasn't always consistent. They may be nice to them today and harsh tomorrow. This leaves hesitant wandering into adulthood in search of constant love. When they are about to start a relationship, vacillators picture the kind of romantic relationship they want to have. When things don't go as planned, even if it began to the way they wanted it to, such lovers will quickly be reminded of their childhood that they may not deserve consistent love. Put differently. It's hard to please these kinds of lovers. You could do all the right things for months, and the very day you fail to impress them, they withdraw and start feeling dejected. The solution to these kinds of lovers is that they need to stop making the ideal form of relationship they want to have. Instead, they should know the person, both the good and bad sides. Lesser expectations will keep their relationship healthy."

The Avoiding Lover

"These kinds of lovers grew up in homes where everyone values their space. Put differently, and privacy was the order of the day. So, when these kinds of lovers get into a relationship, at most times, they just want to be left alone. If they are mad at you, they want to be left alone. It has nothing to do with their partner. They just want to be alone at the moment. Sometimes, in the middle of a conversation with their lover, they might feel the need to withdraw into their space. The best solution to these kinds of lovers is to always share their problems or emotions with their partners, rather than withdrawing."

"Overall, whether we choose to acknowledge it or not, society plays a part in how we love. And it is for this reason. Couples must first understand why their partners act in a particular way. Most of the behaviour we see in our partners, including how they love us, can be traced back to the environment in which they were raised. This now brings us to the issue we're facing in new love."

With that sentence, Dr. Spike finished her talk. "Any questions ?" the Chairman of the session asked the audience.

"Yes, Sir," there was hand raised, and a young, frail woman stood up. She looked to be of Indian origin and said, "I don't have a question as such, but I do want a sort of explanation or clarification of something that has always had me perplexed. So while I have many things to ask Dr. Spike, I want to first ask about an existing situation." The Chair granted her permission and said, "Yes, young woman, please go ahead."

SFO felt good and proud that a young girl of Indian origin was the first to ask a question from the world's renowned psychologist.

"Thank you very much, Dr. Spike, for such a wonderful talk. I am settled in Tanzania, even though my father is of Indian ethnicity. He went there on deputation as a mining engineer, married my mother, and then decided to stay back and make Tanzania our home after the project was over. So, you could say I have been brought up with Afro – Indian values, customs, and traditions. Notwithstanding that, I have been studying here in the US since my graduation. As a result, I get utterly confused amongst so many cultures, traditions, restrictions, etc., that my thinking tends to get clouded at times. To elaborate further, time and again, we are told never to forget our forefathers' values. Yet, we are brought up or always advised to follow a contemporary approach to life. That said, we are never told to follow the past approach of 'Love, which obviously has no borders, develops or builds most passionately, and follows no tradition or set path. So, what are your views on 'Love,' relationships, etc.?"

Dr. Spike looked at this girl with her stunningly beautiful eyes. "To answer your question, I need time, and I do not know if Mr. Chairman would allow that."

There was a big roar in the hall. Then, the crowd started cheering and demanded that more time be allocated to Dr. Spike as almost everyone wanted to ask similar things." The Chairman said that he was happy to oblige only on one condition, that they would have to agree to a reduced lunchtime break from 90 minutes to 30 minutes. The crowd was more than willing. SFO was more than happy, too, as he thought he would get a better insight into Dr. Spike's views.

More from Dr Spike

Dr. Spike realized that the crowd in the hall was energized and waiting for her to continue. There were roaring claps that just would not stop. She bowed her head in gratitude, folded her hands in natural Namaste, and started her talk.

"Now, I shall tell you something which is beyond cultures, castes, nationalities, and all such considerations due to changing perspectives. The world is a global village, and advancements of new technologies have brought people on the same platform." She knew that she was making a wild but loaded statement, but then it was the only way to reach the broadest spectrum in the audience so diverse to start thinking.

"Back in the days, love was romantic. Put differently. Relationships lasted longer than what we have today. Once upon a time, love used to communicate real effort—efforts like two people falling in love, including having their friends help them meet each other or pass on letters or gifts, due to restrictions or limitations of situations/society. The man would send her gifts, especially red roses, in trying to woo her or seek her attention. He would write letters with genuine feelings, hoping to develop the desired fondness in her heart. The persuasion took effort and patience. When they eventually fell in love, both were sure of how to cherish and nourish their love. In short, the olden-time lovers didn't want to give up trying. However, it long it took to convince the other person of their feelings. They knew that deep inside. They had to overcome every obstacle to bring out their true expression of love. And what happened? Their bond was way stronger back then, and the best part is that most of them experienced the happily ever after as a reality. Now, if you haven't noticed, I am talking about the kind of love we had in the 60s, 50s, 70s, even in eightees, etc. Basically the kind of love before the modern age, new love."

Contemporary Love

"Contemporary love is far from having the kind of romance the traditional ones had. Many factors could be attributed to this but let's not start pointing fingers so quickly. Nevertheless, thanks to the advent of the internet, old-school, time-built love is gradually becoming extinct in this instant gratification era. Today, for the most part, people now have their fair share of love online with whoever they meet without actually meeting them. Today, people fall in love without knowing how the person looks as they only see them through various media platforms like Facebook, WhatsApp, etc. From our analysis on love and infatuation that I explained in my talk, if you love another person you've never met but just have a romantic image of them, it is nothing but infatuation."

"As a result, online relationships are now the order of the day. Today's kind of relationship is in the chasm between online (imagery) and actual reality. And how do we communicate our reasoning, emotions, and daily experiences to these people? By texting! Another virtual means of communication."

"Yes, I'm well aware that it is way easy to text someone than going out to meet them in person. But, here is what you need to consider. Why would you choose to text over meeting a person, knowing that either person could well be whoever they want and far away from the reality of who they are! That person could well be wearing a mask they don't want to take off. The virtual world is great but trust me when I say it breeds the fakest set of relationships built on nothing but illusions. Here is the point I am trying to make."

"While it takes little to no effort to meet someone over the internet than doing so in reality, we all need to ask ourselves this personal question. How long do you think an online relationship is going to last? Just be honest with yourself. Are you happy in your online dating world? Don't you ever feel alone even though you have internet love? Regardless of what you may say, online or internet love isn't as fulfilling as reality. This is why this generation complains about being bored to death even when they are in a relationship. Let me also give you an example the same way I did when talking about traditional love. Let's say there is a girl called Saanvi who wants to find a partner. She goes online into one of the popular dating sites and searches for a partner. BOOM! In a split second, she finds one. In about a week or two, they begin dating, and they fall in love. Now, Saanvi is convinced based on the guy's profile, who states that he is tall, handsome, is single, and ready to mingle. Remember, this is a make-believe image based on his profile. In reality, Saanvi only has a perception of whom she is dating."

"Now, what she doesn't know is that the guy she has already fallen for updated a fake profile. Fake in the sense that he's not single. Ideally, he should not be searching, as he has been married for over 14 years and has kids. How is Saanvi supposed to know this? She can't because all their meetings were held virtually. Perhaps the profile also read that he was six feet tall when he was only 5ft 6 inches. Again, how is she supposed to know this when she has never seen him physically to ascertain the accuracy of his height. Things like these and many more are the reasons why contemporary love doesn't last because they are built on pretense and lies. With that said, how is a typical contemporary relationship characterized?"

" But then there are exceptions I shall discuss later."

Meanwhile, SFO was wondering how and from where these experts attain so much knowledge. What was their motivation? Did they actually feel like normal human beings? If they did, it was possibly difficult to be normal. Thinking of this, he smiled because once the Officer had commented to him that normal was not ordinary.

SFO was anxious. He wondered what Dr. Spike would cover next, but whatever it was, he felt she indeed had him captivated. So he was happy as she introduced the subject.

Characteristics of contemporary love

Social Media communication on Internet

There was pin drop silence in the hall, and Dr. Spike continued

"Before we begin to sound ungrateful to what tech has brought to us, I'm sure everyone would attest to the fact that social media has made communication easy for lovers. With numerous social media platforms, you can find yourself talking to a lover who could well be thousands of miles away from you. Plus, this invention has even made the most long-distance relationship feel like they are never apart. However, for every good thing comes a corresponding downside. So, while social media has helped in easy communication, it has killed the need or want of people to communicate verbally. Today, it is not uncommon for lovers to talk for hours on social media, but they wrap off their meeting in 5 minutes when they finally get to meet physically. Whatever is the cause, no one knows but is connected to many platforms, and diversions never focus on the present. All that is important to note is that it is a common scenario in contemporary love."

Orchestrated Relationships

"No matter how hard we try to pay a deaf ear to this, many of today's relationships are just driven by riches, being famous, or holding a high place of authority. No one wants to associate with someone who isn't successful, and that's why there are so many issues in new love. The rate of divorce is on the rise, and so is the rate of domestic violence in relationships. These people never understand what it means to fall in love genuinely. All they do is a trade-off to power and fame, then force themselves to believe they are in love. Relationships are empty these days, and that's a fact."

Love Virtues

"Just as I said, contemporary love feels empty to a large population because most people nowadays fall in love for the wrong reason. He is about to hit a 6-figure contract that makes him an ideal partner. She works for an elite group and looks fashionable, so that makes her an ideal partner. How about, is she a type that can tolerate? Because, for starters, love is patience. As I said earlier, love takes time, and it endures. Yes, they look good and sexy. But can they exhibit the true virtues of love? Why then is it called love? We need to do better and get to a point where people fall in love regardless of their partner's looks or standards. Looks and standards are external. That's for the world to see. Your relationship is for you and your partner to experience. That's why inner virtues are a must. Unfortunately, new love seems to lack these, and that's why unions are falling apart in a year or two. It's almost becoming a norm, and it's quite embarrassing."

As Dr. Spike continued with great clarity, most of the audience did not know how she could touch the most profound chord in their heart and mind. She had that ability. She always knew how to connect with her audience. She knew now it was time to make a comparison.

Why Traditional Love Was/Is better Than Contemporary Love

Tech

"Way back then, lovers never had technology which would have killed the purpose of the love. Put differently. They were not mandated as we are today to call our partners a million times daily just to prove we are in love. Thus, they went about their lives independently and never had to worry about anything until they met. There was no frequent dose of insecurity of having to ask where you were at 3.56 pm when I called, and why didn't you answer! Plus, they weren't always eager to notice if their partner read and replied to their text. Back then, whatever was to be said, had to be said when they met. As a result, dates were never dull as they never ran out of conversations. Dates have different concepts in western and eastern societies. Nevertheless, the underlying concept remains the same. "

Dates

"Today, dates have become so frequent that it has lost the magic touch that it once had. In the 20th century or before, lovers never had the mindset of meeting every day or every weekend. In eastern societies, they met so rarely. This, in turn, made things more special for them. In fact, in some cases, many lovers back then never knew when they'd meet again, literally. This was the very reason why any time they finally had time to meet on a date, be it for 30 minutes, shorter or longer. It felt way special than what we feel today. But, of course, this is logical because it's normal for common items or occurrences to lose their value quickly."

Expectations

"Contemporary love is being demolished daily because of huge expectations. Now, way back then, lovers had a lesser degree of expectation on whoever they were with. When expectations are not met, relationships tend to wash off in a split second. This is why new love is suffering. The bar is so high that it is almost humanly impossible to please some lovers these days. For example, your friend's boyfriend just got your friend (his girlfriend) a new expensive dress; thus, if your boyfriend doesn't do the same, then he doesn't love you, right? Well, no! You just need to stop comparing or have equally huge expectations and instead focus on what you have, as the best."

Privacy

"If there is one known fact about new love is that lovers these days just can't keep to themselves. Everything is announced, and not only does that deprive them of privacy and the chance for people to poke their nose in their affairs, but it also sets the path for a relationship to fail. Things were not like that back then. No one needed to announce to the world what experiences they were having with their lovers. Privacy was often upheld, and it was one of the reasons why love felt genuine. The experiences were real, so there was no need to make their relationship public as quickly as possible."

Intimacy

"Today, intimacy has lost its touch as it is no more highly perceived as before. As we speak, two people could meet up through social media, get to hook up later on without even seeing themselves after that. However, the old traditional love was different."

Being Prudish in Indian Society

"A fascinating phenomenon I wish to tell you is predominantly prevalent in India. In contemporary Indian society, most girls/boys still wish or expect their parents to find a suitable marriage match. That is even if they are involved with someone. They invariably clearly tell this to their dating partners even if they are physically and emotionally involved. Parental approval has a huge role to play. Many of them do have intimate relationships."

There was a big clap and laugh from a sizeable part of the audience that was Indian. That brought a sparkle in the eyes of Dr. Spike. She loved everything that was Indian. SFO's presence was the icing on the cake. He still had that particular clapping style, wherein he would stand and clap long enough for everyone to take notice and, more importantly, win a smile from Dr. Spike. And so, every time he did that, Dr. Spike would give him a unique, loving smile from the podium.

She gave an example of a couple in love where the boy proposed marriage to his girlfriend after one weekend they spent at an exotic resort. The girl simply told him to approach her parents for approval.

Dr. Spike was an expert at judging the mood of her audience. She knew that though she had lots more to say, it was time to start winding down her talk so, she decided to taper off her address with some critical aspects of love

Distractions

"With the social media today and huge demand of instant gratification, distraction has taken over the corner stage of contemporary love. And of course, you can not blame anyone for this because every second, there are lovers who post beautiful pictures online with captions that could take your breath away. While this is great, it distracts other couples who might not reach the same level as those posting the super photos online. Back in the day, love was never under any kind of pressure. It was patient and took its time until a goal was achieved. There was no need for any instant gratification because all they needed was themselves."

Fate

"Trust me. It is way easy to predict the fate of contemporary romantic relationships than the traditional ones. Today, you can easily find two pop artists in a relationship with little to no skill about keeping a relationship. Give it five years, and I promise you it will hit rock bottom. That's how predictable most relationships are today. But, back in the days, no one knew how the relationship would go because even the lovers depended on love to lead them. It wasn't some form of orchestrated destiny for a couple back then. They just lived to enjoy every moment."

She then came to the last point of her session.

Solution

"Now, I must stress this again that I'm in no way trying to shade contemporary love. However, I feel it could do better. There is a need to balance how things are now and how they used to be. For starters, I believe if you want to experience true love in your relationship in these times, it'd be ideal for you to keep your private life private. The whole world doesn't need to know every single thing about your relationship. Instead, that would lead to series of gossips and erroneous beliefs that may damage your relationship. Take, for instance, many former presidents of the United States. For years, even after stepping down from their presidency, you don't find them littering social media with an hourly update of what their family is going through or what the wife does. Although they are rich and famous, they've always believed in keeping things private and looking at how beautiful their marital union is."

"Other than privacy, contemporary love affairs can improve when people start realizing that there is a vast difference between social media conversations and real-life talks. Relationships, most significantly, are solidified when couples get to talk more physically (in person) than online. Constantly talking to your partner through social media could lead to you being short of words when you finally get to meet them in person. Now, here is a sneak peek. You will be with the person physically for eternity when you are married, not just on social media. So, why not develop good verbal communication skills with them right from the start?

This will help you avoid lots of awkward silent moments when you guys will have to sit for minutes without knowing what to say to each other. That's often an embarrassing situation. "

"Overall, we need to understand that love is beautiful when we can explore our options. You can't just be fixated on a particular flow of things and expect the get the best out of love. If you want to know what I mean by exploring your options, then you're going to love what I will talk about next time."

As she ended, she realized, she had the audience in a trance-like state. So, not only did she receive thunderous applause, many in the audience were crying with joy for the topics she covered.

SFO asked her out to a nice Thai dinner at a restaurant on University Avenue to celebrate her award. She readily agreed as she found his attitude, body language, accent, and overall personality, comforting and possibly seducing. She also actually loved the cigarette that SFO smoked. They discussed how she had objectified her research specifically to understand the metamorphosis the Officer was possibly undergoing without telling any of her students why she gave them that topic. Instead, she distributed associated topics to five of her Ph.D. students. Being a reputed Professor, she had a significant research grant, and hence it was easy for her to allocate and spend any amount to reach the bottom of her concerns. Post dinner, SFO escorted Dr. Spike back to her hotel not far from the restaurant. She invited him in for a nightcap. One thing led to another, and they landed up making love through the night.

The next day, Dr. Spike returned to San Fransisco to catch her return flight back to Oslo. They promised to stay in touch as great loving friends!

While on the plane to Oslo, Dr. Spike thought that her feelings, behaviour, and thoughts of love and friendship have transitioned to some extent. She was not even remotely interested or even trying to analyse the why. Finally, however, what she does was write a mail to the Officer.

The Officer was so happy reading the email from Dr. Spike, wherein she had explained the events of the day and her time with SFO. In fact, Officer always longed to read her meaningful, interesting mails. When he read details of her lecture that he received from Dr. Spike, he felt that he would have given Dr. Spike the tightest hug if he was there.

Dr. Spike confessed in the email that her lecture was partly meant to cover the incertitude in the Officer's state of mind. On the other hand, the Officer felt that Dr. Iyengers's memory was undoubtedly not fading away even by a fraction. Officer would often remember that Dr. Iyenger had not spoken to him for two days out of shyness when he kissed her for the first time. Officer could not decipher whether that memory was painful or pleasant. Why she concealed her actual marital status

114

was a thought that still haunted him, more often than not.

Well, Dr. Spike had not mentioned one thing about the night she spent with SFO in her hotel room in the mail to the Officer.

VI
Falling in love with more than one person simultaneously

"Is it possible to love two people at the same time?"
She asked her Mom. "Who do you love? me or Dad ?"
She got her answer.

Smriti Krup

2008

Officer was transferred to Karwar (not far from Goa). He started living with his 'friend' Lieutenant Commander (Lt Cdr) Tej Pratap Singh Chudawat, as Chudwat's wife lived in Vasco Da Gama due to her job. She owned a spa that was doing roaring business. Either one of them would travel approximately 100 km to spend time together on weekends. This Lt Cdr (friend) was a handsome, smart, large-hearted man. He was very well connected with his superiors and would do them favors with gifts, take them out to dinners, etc. Officer and friend used to spend lots of time together and would often discuss life in general, including the deep agony in the Officer's mind in particular. The friend would often advise the Officer to mingle with the opposite sex and have fun to ease that tension in his mind. This friend was very savvy with the internet. While he would surf the net randomly, he would also often surf on Indian dating sites just for fun, as that was something new he had discovered. He used to feel pretty excited as it was

116

so much fun interacting with faceless strangers. He came across a lady living in Papua New Guinea, a small group of islands near the Australian continent. She introduced herself as Seema Gupta. Her husband was posted there on deputation from India. He was a civil engineer working as Head of the project on a setting up of sugarcane processing unit.

One day while chatting with the friend, Seema confessed that she loved men with hairy chests and was fascinated with people in the armed forces. Lt Cdr jumped with joy as he had both these characteristics. He was proud of his hairy chest!

Officer and friend would often laugh about it. One day, the friend confessed to the Officer that he was in love with that lady. "Bloody Idiot you are. How can you love a woman who is already happily married and has two daughters? Moreover, you are happily married and have a gem of a lady as your wife." The friend replied, "I do not know the answer to your 'how'! All I know is that we are in love. Secondly, Seema and her family are moving back from Papua New Guinea to India as her husband's deputation period has expired."

Like always, Officer shared everything with SFO, including the present situation of Lt Cdr and Seema's friendship. On reading the Officer's email, SFO shook his head smilingly and thought that these current generations of Officers should be kicked in their buts. They cannot run ten kilometers. All they want is to fall in love and cherish only that initial feeling. In my time,

117

we never just fell in love but always took love to the next level. Getting intimate and making love with many more women than these idiots can ever imagine was a norm. Suddenly he remembered something. SFO went upstairs in a dirty stinking room and pulled out a handwritten bundle of pages from a closet drawer. This bundle was given to SFO by one of his sailors who wanted to write a book. He had handwritten more than a hundred pages. He had given that bundle to SFO to read. Unfortunately, that sailor died in a fire accident on board a ship, and SFO kept that manuscript with him. He had only glanced through it but not read it thoroughly. He remembered parts of the script and thought the information contained would make good sense to the Officer's friend. So SFO sent that manuscript to the Officer and asked him to hand it over to his friend.

The friend was fond of reading. Within minutes of reading the manuscript, he realized that the sailor was writing a book and had done some astonishing research. Evidently, he wanted to write few articles on the subject and probably would have compiled those in a book form.

The written material started as ;

"Being in love with two people at the same time? Before I discuss the basics here, I will assume that you are one of three types of people reading this book.

1.You feel like you are in love with more than one person, and it is confusing you. You're not quite sure whether you are doing the right thing or should be feeling guilty.

2. You are in love with someone who has told you that they are in love with someone else as well. With this, you just can't seem to wrap your head around it.

3. You are looking forward an open relationship where you can explore your options and have the best of partners."

How true, declared Lt Cdr to the Officer and read some of the written material to the Officer with great interest.

From his heart and feelings of his natural perception and understanding of the phenomenon of love, the sailor had written. His close ones probably knew that he wrote from the heart and had tremendous psychic abilities to decipher many complicated aspects of life.

The sailor wrote: "Now, based on this analysis, I'll be looking to answer the question considering these standpoints. But first, let's address the issue generally. Here is what you should know. The feeling of being in love is no more than the fact that your heart is open, your sexual energy is available, and those two mixings. When your heart's available, you'll feel in love, and when your sexual energy mixes with that, you get that irresistible, that attraction, that aliveness feeling within you. And that feeling of being in love. So what's the answer to the question? Being in love is not an action. It's not something that you do. It's simply a state of 'being.' Expressing your love, being in a relationship, showing your passion, displaying your love is an action. With that said, you can simultaneously love more than one person at the same time. So if you happen to fall under the first category, where you feel like you are in love with more than one person, it's confusing, and you don't know if it could be real if you're feeling it. So the simple answer is: it's real, and there is nothing to feel bad about."

"So fascinating, and what clarity." exclaimed the friend.

Further, the sailor wrote, "If you fall under the second category where you're in love with somebody and they are telling you that they're also in love with someone else. Then you're confused, and you don't think it could be real. Yes, it can be real. And what might be coming up for you is a sense of worthlessness, inadequacy, insecurity, etc. So, I'm going to throw out a hypothetical situation here: Let's say I'm in love with you, and I tell you that I'm also in love with someone else. That doesn't mean that I love you any less. That doesn't mean that you're any less special to me. I may have fallen in love with someone else, but that doesn't make me any less connected to you. As a matter of fact, I may be more connected, more aligned with you. There's so much more to love than what people usually think. Usually, we say I'm in love, and that just bottles up everything, but there's so much more to it than just being in love. There's exploring love. There's being committed. There's alignment. I might fall in love with someone but feel that there's no alignment, and I might not explore anything with them. All it was, was my heart, my sexual

120

energy being open to this other person. It could have just happened during a conversation. This falling-in-love feeling would be more of a natural occurrence if we weren't so closed off. But when you say, I fell in love with another person, and I'd like to explore a connection with them, that's a different thing."

The friend's mind was never amazed as much before. He wished he could have met that sailor who had so much clarity about love. He was convinced that those texts were written for him only. He continued reading.

"If you happen to fall under the third category where you're looking to explore open relationships. Then you should. It is not bad, and it's all about communication. The bottom line is that if you feel like you're in love with someone else, you feel like it's something you need to honor and explore. Or if you are in love with someone who has told you that they are also in love with someone else and feel it's something they need to honor and explore. Here is a word of advice: whatever you do. However, you choose to examine or allow the other person to explore, do it with integrity, be honest, be transparent about what you're feeling, what you're going through, both of you, all of you. Just do it with integrity."

Yes, that I agree, thought the friend. He was convinced that being in love with someone in addition to his wife was not unethical at all. There was no loss of love with his wife. He could never hurt her as he loved her so much, and surprisingly, the lady with whom he connected over the net also thought the same way. She

121

was deeply in love with her husband and daughters. Yet, she also fell in love with this friend and felt deeply attached to him.

The friend was creating his logic from those handwritten pages.

"If you fall into the first category, remember that just because you fell in love, and you've opened up to someone, doesn't mean you need to explore anything with that other person. You can simply honor the internal feeling that you are experiencing. And if you fall into the second category, and this type of situation does not feel right to you, and it doesn't sit well with you even after honestly exploring it internally and discussing it with an open heart, it's not something that you have to go ahead with."

Meanwhile, Seema had confided her developing situation with Lt Cdr, with one of her white Australian friends who had no qualms about open relationships. The Australian directly told Seema that Indians have too many taboos, even though it was Indians who taught the world the art of love. Ancient temples and Kamsutra are great examples, but even then, she said, "You all are hypocrites." The Australian lady would often joke with her friend. "Go to India, spend some quality time with that Indian lover of yours, and come back refreshed." Both of them would laugh aloud. The Australian lady shared some of her thoughts with Seema and said,

Monogamy

"Can people be monogamous? Yes! We can be monogamous regardless of the biological arguments that are made for the opposite. This isn't being pro monogamy - I'm neither for nor against monogamy. It's about where you are and what you feel deep down. You need to experience tapping into the deepest levels of experience here on earth and for the evolution of yourself as a being. Can you be in a relationship Seema, which is different than being in love, simultaneously?"

Australian lady was candid. "Yes! However, with the collective consciousness on this planet right now and us being so heavily identified with this personality, being in a committed relationship or exploring love with one person is enough to bring up many insecurities that we need to look at, face, and face work on. When we open that up to more than one person, it brings even more of that. It is why I said, I support whatever path you take to tap and explore."

She said, "Open up the deeper aspects of yourself; to become the highest being that you can and to experience the most beautiful aspects of relationship and love. You can explore a relationship, an authentic relationship with two people at the same time. Set aside time and space to open up your heart, really share what's going on within you, and allow the other person to express what's going on within them from an authentic space. Now, let's say you've agreed to give it a try. How can you handle falling in love with more than one person at the same time?"

"I shall explain, as I have been through this more than once in my life, and those were beautiful experiences. I still cherish them, and if there is an opportunity again, I shall not back out," and she smiled with a wink. Both laughed aloud.

Seema thanked her Australian friend profusely as she felt her guilt reduced and, she was getting more and more clarity. She also liked that feeling of approval immensely. The Australian continued.

How to Handle Falling in Love with Two People

"Here is the thing about loving simultaneously. While it is surely possible, you need to tread carefully. How? You need to kill whatever intimate urge that may arise while you're with your current partner. If you feel uncomfortable, then you need to be honest and open up to your partner. In that case, you will be risking losing one or both. You've got to be sure of yourself and should be able to handle these two as independent attachments—no interference amongst each other. Love is not infidelity. It is being real with another and not going behind anyone's back. With that said, do you know how you can manage multiple love exploration and how do they differ?"

Teased Seema, "No, I don't know but what I do know is that you are a bloody great experienced lady."

Australian laughed at the compliment and said, "I believe you are only aware of this present and one life. So better enjoy and cherish it but ensure that you don't hurt anyone. That will be criminal. Much more than hurting anyone who has not done anything."

"You should be a Love guru," Seema said as she laughed. Then, she asked the Australian lady to explain things to her more structured and straightforwardly. Australian lady was too happy to oblige.

Seema was aware that she was getting more comfortable with her loving Lt Cdr friend in India. They were much more intimate and would chat much more often on messengers, including webcam. Therefore anything her Australian friend told her would only help her clarify any doubts.

The Australian love expert started to explain the answer to the question she asked Seema.

How Do They Differ?

"Before you begin thinking that you love your new-found love more than your current partner, you should understand that love is often always fun and exciting at the beginning. So, you might just be experiencing that. Also, think, what is it that you like in the person more than your partner? Only their looks? If that's the case, then know it's ultimately going to be heading nowhere. Just analyze the (partner vs. friend) differences and make your choice based on who makes you happy. If you're hiding something from your partner, it means you may be having an emotional affair. Personally speaking, I approve of that. There is no harm. All parties are happy." That made good sense, thought Seema as she continued to listen while the Australian continued

Think about your needs and wants

"Most cultures tend to value monogamy both emotionally and physically. However, you may want and need different things out of a relationship. Do you feel you need to be emotionally invested in one person at a time? Some people only want to focus on one person, while many find their capacity to impart love simultaneously. But, you should know that romantic or otherwise, love is not finite. Think about how loving two people make you feel. Do you feel exhausted by it or invigorated? Is it something you feel guilty about, or do you feel comfortable with the fact you love two different people? Identify what you need. Do you want to love simultaneously or one after the other? This is a crucial reality you need to come to terms with. The most important aspect is never to feel guilty. Never ever! It is your choice. No one has the right to judge. Love is non-judgemental. There are no rights or wrongs. It is only your perception that will decide what is right and what could be wrong. So just go with your instinct. Do not feel any negativity. "The Australian could feel the intensity of Seema's interest, so she continued

Consider your take on emotional monogamy

"You may need to be loyal to one person on an emotional level as well as a physical one. For others, emotional monogamy is not necessary. You can be physically faithful to one person but can have feelings for people outside your certified relationship. For some, the ability to love one person at a time is vital to a happy relationship. For others, loving simultaneously is also possible. Now, not everyone shares this sentiment or ability in the same way. And monogamy isn't for the set of people who don't take love as a finite value. Instead, consider pursuing a relationship with both parties at the same time. Keeping your expectations open."

Seema was so relieved. Yes, she was undergoing precisely a similar situation, and so was her net lover in India. The Australian lady sorted the jumbled thoughts and doubts in her mind, especially, "How to handle your current relationship when in love with another person at the same time?"

Seema wanted to know more about the aspects of an affair. The Australian said.

Consider whether you're having an emotional affair

"If you're currently in a relationship, loving two people can never pose problems if you and your partner have good self-love and satisfaction amongst yourselves. You will be open to giving one another adequate space and not interfering with each other's respective normal life. It also boils down to deep respect for another person. But, on the other hand, being in love with another person could constitute an emotional affair. This could cause feelings of pain and betrayal for your current partner, especially if there is a lack of understanding. So, look for any signs that may show that you're having an emotional affair. If that's the case, you may feel the need to justify your behavior and ensure no latent guilt. On the other hand, you may also feel the need to cover your tracks. Do you feel excited when you know you get to see this person? If so, that's a sign it's emotional bonding. The emotional bond is a beautiful feeling and hurts no one if handled well."

"And again, I say. One has to be non-judgemental. There are no rights or wrongs. If you go by societal norms, you will get confused and stressed. Every society has its dos and don'ts. You must go by what makes you happy without creating any trace of unhappiness for anyone else."

Talk to your partner only if you feel comfortable doing so

"However, if you are not comfortable in speaking with your partner, it would be wise to spare the possible agony. Even if you have a small hint of unhappiness creeping in, hold your horses dear."

"How do you attempt this? First, pick the right time to talk and eliminate distractions when you have the discussion. Second, make sure you turn off phones and computers and are basically in a relaxed state of mind. Third, whatever you decide, make sure you set clear boundaries that both you and your partner have to agree to and fully understand. If you don't set bounds or have a good understanding, be sure the discussion will spiral out of control."

Discuss your feelings

"Who are the best persons to discuss your inner feelings with" Asked Seema. "The best is to keep those to yourself. But you Indian women have an inadequacy of self-love. Hence the need for some kind of approval." She laughed. "The best would be to discuss with your non-judgmental friend, and in case that is not enough, a good therapist will do." She smiled as she replied.

Polyamorous Relationship

"Now, if I tell you something, do not be surprised. It does happen. It happens all over. In your Indian societies too. I know all this as I too was part of such arrangement once." While Seema gasped in wonder, the Australian just winked and continued

About Polyamory

"Polyamorous people are open to having multiple romantic relationships at once, as long as all parties consent to this kind of romance. People who are polyamorous do not feel monogamy is necessary to a happy and fulfilling relationship. Polyamory is not a choice. There are many ways to figure out if you're polyamorous. Now, look back on your relationships. Was dating one person enough to fulfill your emotional desires? Or did you always find yourself looking for

129

love elsewhere? If that's the case, the latter, you may be polyamorous. There is some stigma against polyamory, so work to shut that out. Remember when it comes to relationships, one size does not fit all."

Boundaries

"Boundaries are always crucial in a relationship and especially so if you're in love simultaneously with more than one person. You need to state vividly or diplomatically to them the boundaries none of them can cross. It's their choice whether to accept it or not. If you're looking into an open or semi-open relationship, make sure that you live up to your comfort level. Never ever cross that. Would you like to be physically intimate with both parties? Can your partners pursue relationships outside of their romance with you? These are questions you need to ask when proceeding with an open relationship. If your partner at the time is entirely against such a relaxed affair, reach out to the other lover and make sure you know the kind of contact you're allowed to have or what sort of contact."

"That is so bloody difficult." Exclaimed Seema with despair. Her friend retorted, "Then forget about your net lover in India. You should not proceed with your Indian net lover. In case you feel you are truly in love with him or even have some positive feelings towards him, then be confident that you will be able to handle all that would come along with another package of love." But more importantly, never forget, "You live only once."

Seema goes back to India

While Lt Cdr was delighted that he would finally meet Seema in person, Seema herself was full of anxieties. Seema took some time to settle in her new house, new surroundings, etc. They finally decided to meet at his friend's house about three weeks after she landed in India. Within no time of the meeting, both struck an excellent chord. Whether they knew their boundaries, that is, if there were any; neither was sure. However, they would meet as convenient to both. There were no compulsions, no sad moments in their relationship. On the contrary, they were delighted to be with each other, which was why the Lt Cdr was so relaxed and yet amazed.

As always, the Officer told SFO of these developments and wondered how easily the Lt Cdr could get another person in his life while he was still entangled in thoughts of Dr. Iyengar. SFO laughed aloud and said. "You will not improve," he retorted. "You idiot, how many times do I have to tell you that Dr. Iyenger is gone? Throw her out of your system. Look after your wonderful wife, or/and have an affair. Then, if you think I am wrong, see how happy your friend is."

Officer felt emotional as Dr. Iyengar's name was spoken and yet smiled. Yes, he loved his wife, but Dr. Iyenger was so unique that his fond memories with her would still trouble him and make him miss her. And many times, he would feel depressed.   He would then fondly remember Dr. Spike's sermon on the Psychology of love and draw some solace from what he learned from those interactions. He also believed that one day they would meet again, and he would ask her more questions!

131

To date, in all the interactions, message exchanges, etc. Officer had with SFO, and latter was secretive enough not to spill any beans of what happened in Palo Alto on that beautiful night, post-dinner, on the award day.

VII
Social Media and Love

"My eyes search only for your name whenever I open social media .."

Quotes Diary

2011

Major Defence Exhibition in Paris

"You connect with me on Facebook," said Margaret. "I understand that Facebook (FB) is very addictive and time-consuming, possibly tedious to operate by someone like me, unaware of such platforms." said the Officer at a stall of a very big defence company. Indian Navy had deputed the Officer to visit a major defence exhibhition in Paris. He was chatting with this beautiful French damsel manning one of the stalls at the exhibition. He liked her style, the way she spoke, and hence was lightly flirting with her. Margaret was a 21-year-old student of Management and was employed by a defence company to man their stall for five days. She was surprised that the Officer was not on FB. She laughed aloud and told him of all the subtleties and advantages of FB. She showed him how to connect with people, share pictures, communicate much more efficiently and more interestingly than regular emails, etc.

Officer Joined Facebook

He was amused as he joined FB the same night and commenced learning how to operate his newly created account. SFO joined as well. Dr. Spike smiled when the Officer wrote her an email explaining his newfound interest.

The Officer would now carry his laptop wherever he went and, at the slightest chance, would open his FB account and start browsing. He connected with his school mates distant cousins and was so happy to know from one of his classmates that she had a crush on him while in the fifth grade. Both laughed it off. There were so many motivational messages that he loved. The majority of boys in his class in school were well settled. Two were still bachelors in their early forties. Then there were two of his girl classmates who had divorced their husbands. One was a spinster, and one had been widowed. It would give him great pleasure to interact with all of them. His friend's list grew over time. Then he realized that there were groups created by like-minded people. So he was added to a couple of groups. There he started interacting with many unknown people. He liked some but did not like many. He was a good communicator, and many loved his comments for humor and spontaneity.

As for SFO, he got very popular as an agony aunt to many. Being an internet platform, no one knew how much he would be stinking due to the obnoxious cigarette he smoked. When the Officer discussed the advantage of being in a virtual environment with SFO, they both had a good laugh.

Swami Iyer was already very active on FB. One day he mentioned something of a philosophical nature to the Officer.

"Social media, without a doubt, has given us the luxury to enjoy life to its fullest. Thanks to social media platforms, we can capture every moment and either choose to keep it for memory's sake or share it with the world to see. It gets even better when people like, comment, and share our post as the world becomes flat." "Now, that's that for the basics. Regarding relationships, social media platforms have made it possible for lovers to have the time of their lives even when they are not together through skype, zoom, etc., and can even text each other at any time. So, while social media platforms have undoubtedly blessed us with all these, there is some not-so-bright side to it as well. Social media use, especially by lovers, has some adverse effects on love. Without pondering a lot about it, let me give you the reasons."

The Officer wondered as to why Swami Iyer had to dissect everything so minutely and carry out research. Why could he not enjoy the best things of life that are connected with the advent of this technology? But then that was Swami Iyer. Those were the traits that made him unique. The Officer always wanted to listen to him as Iyer would say everything in highly lucid narration.

He would find himself engaged every time Swami Iyer made a point.

Swami Iyer continued his sermon on Skype with the Officer on the adverse of love through social media. He said

The adverse effect of social media on relationship

"Now, before we kick start the discussion, I'd love to start by emphasizing something. I personally don't believe that social media in and of itself will be what makes or breaks a love relationship. However, the habits that we have and that we create, especially around how we spend our time and attention on social media, can definitely lead to problems. Here are the top three reasons why social media is affecting love adversely."

Before Iyer could speak further, Officer smiled to himself, seeing the passion of Iyer, and continued to listen carefully. Officer knew that Iyer's conversation always made a lot of sense, and he had an exciting way to communicate his thoughts.

Old Flames

"Social media opens up the possibility to reconnect with old flames or to start new ones. What do I mean by this? You may not even realize it at first, but on Facebook, whatever friends you have are those with whom you either reconnect or those whom you connect by either liking each other's pictures or comments. Those comments turn into more comments of a personal nature, which can turn into personal messages. At first, you will feel it's all innocent. It's all online anyway; however, when you begin to notice yourself hiding what you're doing from your spouse or begin to do things in secret, it's a cause for red flags. Why? The only reason you will hide something from your loved one is that either you know your loved one will not understand, or you are not sure if something that you are doing is right as such, and if so, then you may want to check yourself in what you're doing."

Comparison

"The next thing about the excessive use of social media is that you'll start comparing your close ones to someone else or comparing your life to someone else's. And what happens when you do this? You become dissatisfied with what you have. Many studies suggest a link between an increase in social media usage and a decrease in marital satisfaction. What does that mean? The more time a lover spends on Facebook, whatever it might be, the less happy they are with their relationship. So, if you want to lead a content and happy life, reduce your level of social media usage. It's not hard to be lured into the comparison trap, and when you're analyzing their highlights and best moments against your real behind-the-scenes life, it will seem like you're on the losing side every time. But, trust me, you're not. The grass may look greener on the other side, but that's just because it's sitting on top of a sewer."

Officer thought, when does this Iyer guy get time to think about all this. He was in awe of Iyer's excellent understanding of the subject and his ability to put across everything with great simplicity.

Officer's popularity on FB was increasing day by day, especially with ladies. He was handsome, and it showed in his profile picture. They were drawn towards the Officer for his confident look, uniform, and the works. Topped with that, he had a subtle knack to make witty comments that impressed many women as they thought he had good intellect. He made many friends of both genders, all over the world. He never ridiculed anyone. His great sense of humor was his biggest asset. When he was with Dr. Iyenger, he never felt the existence of any other woman. Now he felt happy that women of all age groups were attracted to him as bees get attracted to flowers.

He loved to comment on many posts and learned a lot about human beings, which was the Officer's primary intent. Human behaviour and allied subjects. He was amused at how people took social media so seriously.

One day in the course of normal conversation, Swami Iyer claimed that social media was harming society. Officer knew that Iyer typically never uttered anything without meaning or conviction. Sure enough, Iyer explained what he meant.

Kills Love

"This is the most devastating thing an excessive use of social media can cause to lovers. Also, it's perhaps the least suspecting. Now, here is how it kills love." explained Swami Iyer.

"The more time you spend on social media, the less time you're spending with your lover. How many times have you been in a situation where you and your partner were at dinner, or you were sitting at home talking on the couch? More than likely, either you or your partner were just focusing deeply on your phone throughout that dinner. How does that make you feel? Now think about that occurring every time. You may be together in the same physical space, but you aren't together. You aren't talking. You aren't interacting. Over time, you guys will start growing apart, and love will be no more. You need that interaction and communication in a relationship. You even need eye contact to reassure your partner that the love is here to stay. Quite frankly, the health and the longevity of your relationship depend on good and proper communication. So, examine your habits. How are you spending your time? Do you find yourself looking at your phone on social media more than you are connecting and interacting with your lover? If so, then you may want to make some changes, and if you're thinking - but I don't like spending time with my lover, we don't have anything to talk about anymore; then you need to balance things up immediately before it becomes too late."

How to balance it

Officer realized that Swami Iyer had a point and innocently asked how to balance that.

Notification

"No matter how focused you are in life, no matter how deep your level of concentration is, constantly receiving buzzes from your phone is certainly going to cause distraction. There is absolutely no doubt about this. Now, think of it this way. You never can tell when a friend is going to ping you. You're never aware when that long-anticipated email is going to come into your mailbox. All these things could come simultaneously, or one after the other, and you will be highly tempted to get hold of your phone. And once you do that, guess what's going to follow? Yes, you guessed right – you are going to be distracted. The rest is going to be history, as you'll keep navigating from one app to the other. So, what should you do? Turn off those buzzes or any notifications. That way, you won't know when any notification comes into your phone. If you want to take things a bit further and as a smartphone user, you can simply turn off background app refresh under 'settings.' This will stop the automatic synchronization of those notifications into your phone; meaning you won't be bugged by any notification that unexpectedly comes into your device. If you're an Android user, you can do the same, except this time, you'll need to toggle the "sync" option off not to receive notifications immediately."

Officer smiled and thought. "How does this Madrasi know so much?" he thought. Officer would invariably address all South Indians as 'Madrasis' and every beautiful lady as 'Madrasan.' That would also make him

140

feel deeply connected to Dr. Iyenger, and he loved that feeling. Officer could operate modern apps with ease but was not as thorough as Iyer or as many of his lady friends on social media.

His thought process got interrupted by the deep voice of Swamy Iyer asking him to focus on what he was saying and stop dreaming!

PC/Laptop

"Another way to indirectly reduce your usage of social media is to try doing so from your personal computer (PC). So, delete all the social media apps from your phone and log them in on your laptop. Whenever you feel like going online, retrieve your computer from wherever you have kept it and log in. Please do this for 21 days until it becomes a habit. At that time, you'll discover that the thought of having to find where you have kept your laptop, wait for it to boot, log in with passwords, etc., will discourage you from always wanting to go online. The fact is that social media has become very addictive because our mobile phones are always handy, and it is effortless to log on to any of these social media platforms. So, the aim here is to try and make the whole process at least a little complicated. Doing this over time will eventually derail your mind from going online too often because our brain has been conditioned such that it doesn't like things that stress us or make us work extra. Most times, when you think of the whole process itself, you'll lose interest."

The Officer always discussed Iyer's lectures with Dr. Spike. She would often laugh aloud and also wonder how this Iyer guy knows so much about psychology without formal education in the subject. She would have loved to take him as a Ph.D. student under her.

However, Iyer so passionately continued to educate Officer

Decision

"Another way to reduce or balance your time on and off social media is to make a firm decision. Everything in life starts with a decision. Say to yourself, or you can even make it a mantra, that no matter what, you're never going to spend more than a stipulated amount of time on social media platforms. Do this and build your discipline over time. It is going to help you as well as the partner in your life. It will allow you to come to terms with the fact that there is time for everything in life. There is time for social media, yes, and there is a time where you should be spending hours with your partner. And the time spent with your partner should be greater than the amount of time you spend on social media. So, make the decision and curb your time on these platforms."

Pitfall

"One more way to trick your mind into staying off most or balancing your time on social media is to make it believe all the dangers of spending too much time looking at other people's feeds. Instead, you need to understand that too much time spent on these platforms can lead to things like depression, sadness, and discontent. These dangers are lethal enough to cause problems to your brain. So, always be conscious of this fact whenever you are about staying on these platforms for too long."

Widgets

"Never allow any social media application to be included in any of your widget or home screen. This is because allowing these apps there will tempt you to click on them. So you want to take them away from your site as far as possible. Perhaps you could create subfolders and just stack them there. Better still, you can rename the folder as "junk" so that at first glance, your mind won't be interested in finding out what is in the folder."

Rules For Social Media and Relationship

"Social media is a colossal part of our day to day lives. It has gotten so deep into people that some even use it as a job. Whatever the case, maybe, you know we use it to communicate; and just to talk to someone. Instead of sending a text, we use it to meet people. We use it to date, and needless to say, it's not going anywhere. So, what does this mean? It means that we need to ensure that some rules and boundaries are in place; it doesn't negatively affect the people we love or our relationships. If that's what you want, then here are five rules that I really believe need to come into play when it comes to dating relationships and social media."

What a brilliant man this Iyer is sighed the Officer in his mind. He used to get so many of these questions in his mind but could never think of a practical solution, and here, one monk-like Madrasi was explaining mythology and social media with the same ease. What a genius. Indeed Iyer was a genius. When he got involved in a subject, he explained it with a deep sense of passion, and time flew so fast. Iyer went on to explain further.

Privacy

"Given the age we are in where everything seems only to thrive in public, you need to try and keep your relationship private. However, to keep it hidden or otherwise is strictly your choice based on many factors. What I mean by this is there is a huge difference between privacy and secrecy. By keeping your relationship private, you're openly telling people that you are in a relationship. It's changed in your status feed, and you've got a few photos up. However, you're not divulging every single intricate detail. So, that way, there's still an element of privacy to what's going on between you and your partner. If your relationship is hidden, you deny publicly that you are in a couple of relationships. This is like an invite to other people to try and encroach on your partner or yourself. After all, they think you're single, which means more temptation. You don't have to post about it every second, like where you went shopping with your spouse, the food you're eating at the moment, etc. There is no need to display your emotions more than necessary. These are very private between two individuals and unique every time, and that's a beauty of a relationship. It has to be cherished by those who are living it and not a matter to display or talk about openly."

Stretching it further, Iyer said

Your Dirt

"The second rule you should keep to while trying to save your relationship from being hurt by social media is by not airing your dirty laundry online. What do I mean by this? If you're going through some issues, let's say a bitter fight. If the person was maybe acting like an idiot during the weekend, the whole world does not need to know. Why? First, it actually doesn't really help when it comes to showing that you have self-respect and you feel that you can advertise to the world what's going on in your head and your heart. Put differently, the more you try to shame a person online, the sillier you'll look. It will just make you appear as a bitter person or immature. So, it's best to go through some things in private, or you could place a call to one of your best friends or family members and share it with them. It's better to keep it off social media, especially for personal issues, no matter how tempting it is. Another reason you should not post such things online is that it will invite unwanted opinions into your life, not just in your life but in your relationship. The more people know about it, the more people will talk and give opinions about it. So, make sure you refuse such 'urges' at all times."

So deep and so true, thought the Officer. When he conveyed this conversation to Dr. Spike, she was also spellbound with the maturity of Swami Iyer. However, Swami Iyer was not finished

Time For Everything

"Another rule is for you to be disciplined enough to know when to switch off from social media. And when I mean switch, I'm talking like literally turning off your phone. You see, a lot of the time, we're so busy looking down at our screens or on the computer or constantly checking our Instagram, Facebook, Snapchat, whatever that may be. Plus, there's a new app every day, so we can become incredibly busy with social media such that we forget to prioritize our partner or our relationship. So, try to have some rules such as not looking at your social media first thing in the morning; instead, talk to your partner and not bring your phones or iPads to the table or maybe even consider switching off all electronic devices and social media access at a specific time at night so that you can have some quality 'our time' together. This will help ensure that the bond between you two only gets stronger. Contrary to this, once your partner begins to feel like you're more interested in being on social media platforms than with them, it will start breeding some negative vibes around you guys, and that might not end well over time. So, be disciplined enough to know when to turn off your phones and go off social media."

Comparison

"Don't compare yourself and your relationship to what you see on social media. You might be hearing this all the time but trust me, most of the time, the couples you see always looking happy and attached online don't always maintain the same energy of the camera. No one comes online to post when they have fought with their partner. No one comes online to show the world how they cursed either so severely during an argument that they started destroying stuff at home. All you'll see is the lovey-dovey moments where they hold hands, go shopping, etc. This is where you need to understand. It's all been filtered. It's all about marketing. People aren't going to put the bad stuff, but it doesn't mean that bad stuff isn't happening. When you keep viewing these things over time, you can get transcend into a false world by thinking that the grass is greener on the other side because of the positivity of what we see. No, it's not. You need to understand that the grass is greener where you water it.

Here is the thing; what is going on may not be the reality of what you see or read, so control yourself when you feel like you're starting to compare yourself. You could

146

be better off than half those people you see online, and I'm saying that as a fact."

Swami Iyer was never tired while lecturing. He was always so involved when he spoke. The Officer continued to listen to him with great enthusiasm.

Temptations

"Truth is, social media brings temptation. So make sure when you use social media, use it concerning yourself, your partner, and your relationship. What do I mean by this? This means that you shouldn't follow or like certain accounts on FB because those are overly suggestive or have sexualized images and may not be respectful to your partner. It also means that when certain people invite you, you will have to say no."

"Look, don't think that it's about all you do not want to offend someone. It's more important that you don't disrespect or offend the person you're actually in love with or dating, rather than a random stranger to whom you have absolutely no connection. You've got to be aware there will be temptations. People from your past will try and connect with you again because they can now have this access that was not there ten years ago. So, you need to be aware of this temptation, and you've got to be aware of what is going on as per your actions and your usage of social media. Don't ever make your partner feel like your disrespecting them because of it. That is how you build trust, and it's also how you keep your relationships strong and healthy."

Swami Iyer ended his call with the Officer and told him I now want you to think of what I have said.

Days passed by. By now Officer was armed with good information on the good and bad effects of social media. The dos and donts. How to handle FB, Instagram, Whatsapp, Twitter, etc., etc. All these platforms had their advantages and disadvantages. Their norms. Officer was a member of numerous groups ranging from bhajan (spiritual) groups to schoolmates, college mates, Psychology, sports, and many more groups. He loved being a part of those and was exceedingly popular. He also started getting along with some of the people based on mutual interests. He was awed by some, and likewise, some were smitten by his charm. He was amazed to realize that, at heart, every age group had similar aspirations that were to remain connected somehow. Officer had a large circle of friends, including those on social media. In classic terms, most of these so-called friends were at best acquaintances or good acquaintances. He did have an admirable personality, and most thought they liked being close to the Officer. His behaviour was full of warmth and compassion.

Officer would often remember words of his social science teacher that man was a social animal. Men and women yearn to be accepted by society. Officer's job entailed traveling all over the country and also internationally. He would often connect with exciting people on FB. Some would exchange phone numbers too, and the advent of WhatsApp revolutionized the way people across the world communicated. That proved suitable for the Officer as he was a great communicator. He could connect with the feelings of the ones who were close to him. No wonder that Dr. Iyenger was so profoundly attracted and attached to the Officer. Officer, too reciprocated every emotion of hers. Her memories still haunted him. He had not shared that part of his life with anyone except SFO, Dr. Spike, and Swami Iyer. By now, they all had connected on WhatsApp and formed a separate group where they would often chat. Dr. Spike and Swami Iyer were great at lecturing. SFO would just use smile emojis when such discussions happened between Dr. Spike, Iyer, and the Officer.

On the other hand, SFO still believed that the Officer would come out of his deep-seated gloom whenever he made love with a genuinely passionate woman. Officer would always laugh at his belief. He was a devoted husband. Many times he felt like sharing everything with his wife. But, then, he would stop just short of it. It wasn't easy to share his state of mind lest she misunderstands and spoilt their relationship for a person who was no more.

On the social media groups, the Officer found an interesting pattern. There were jokes. Motivational quotes mostly forwarded posts and umpteen such forwards. Officer would always wonder how people had so much time to spend on social media. Then there were group politics. Many crossed limits and were blocked. Officer enjoyed all that and would often flirt and tease some in the group in a very light healthy way. Yet, he never touched or commented upon anyone's dignity, never crossed his limits, appeared chivalrous even through his posts, and that won him more and more lady friends.

The Officer was delighted when he somehow reconnected with a lady whom he knew very well a long time back. She was the wife of a superior Officer he respected a lot and had lost touch with many years ago. Now they had all settled in UAE. Through another FB group, he learned that one of the ladies in that group would travel from the USA to India every year to have a good time with her ex-boyfriends. Another lady from Spain left her family to be with her lover in the US but was forced to head back home when she learned that her lover was embroiled in a drug controversy. Then, this semi-psycho man in Lucknow fell in love with his singing partner lady residing in Denmark. It was routine for them to fight and make up online, for everyone in the group also knew precisely what was going on. However, their relationship ended when this semi-psycho man posted some of her nude pictures. There were so many exciting stories, and the Officer could pass a fair amount of his time reading or being part of all this gossip.

Deep inside, the Officer was never interested in strengthening those newly found bonds. He was polite and decent and would often have a lot of fun with his social media friends through all kinds of banter. However, one expression that irritated the Officer to no end was 'hmmm." He hated to read this as it seemed like a blank expression as it conveyed nothing whatsoever from the person writing this.

One day the Officer realized that he was intrinsically drawn to a lady member of one particular group. She was quite different from other members. Her name was Reshma Kandwal. She was a regular contributor, and through her profile picture, the Officer felt she had uniquely beautiful Indian looks as seen in the Himalayan areas. Her English was not the best, but her expression was excellent. She could convey her mind with her superb choice of simple words, which were invariably not commonly used when trying to express one's thought process. Officer found that very cute and often teased her lovingly to use those words. She would laugh and laugh and often blush whenever the Officer jokingly and lovingly asked her to express herself using those words. They would comment on each other's posts and, at times, joke and tease each other on a wide range of topics. They would ardently wait for each other's comments, remarks, pictures, stories, etc., on FB and various other social media.

Some of the lines or messages written were short one-liners like ….

*"A cartoon like me
A fool like me
Apne number banane ki jarurat nahi (Don't try to impress me)
I know better about myself
Ha ha ha......
No need to be smart
This time not possible
I am a normal person who knows nothing.
Some people think their wives are devils
No one knows me
Jhagda ho jayega (A misunderstanding might happen)
Agar gussa ho gayee tou aap manna Lena (If I ever lose my cool, make sure you cajole me)
As such
I will try
He he
Relax
Don't think so much
I feel awkward
You are impossible at times
Your handshake gave so much of warmth and nice feeling"*

She was far different from all he ever met. She would very often tease the Officer of his numerous lady connections and how women appreciated his comments on a particular group. Very mild jealousy probably triggered that tease. Although Reshma never agreed to that, Officer reduced his flirting so as not to offend Reshma. He just wanted to see her happy all the time.

Over a period of time, they developed a very healthy bond and liking for each other. While Dr. Spike named this budding bond as 'Fondness,' SFO named it 'Foolishness.' However, Swami Iyer knew that there was something very deep behind all these developments and called it 'Special.' Swami was very confident that there was something unique about this friendship and believed timings of nature. He strongly opined that events would unfold something at the right time as ordained by Universe, God, or Nature. In the end, whatever anyone called the bond did not matter because all that mattered was indeed the groundwork for the connection that seemingly had been laid.

VIII
Reincarnation, Soulmates, Twinflames

"And I'd chose you; in hundred of lifetimes, in a hundred worlds, in any version of reality, I'd find you and I'd chose you."

Chaos of stars

2014

Moscow

The plane landed in Moscow. Officer was so delighted to be there. Russia, especially St. Petersburg, was one of his dream places. However, this time his work was in Moscow city. He always preferred to take the Moscow express train to travel from the airport to Moscow city. He simply loved that journey for its breathtaking panorama. It always reminded him of one of the most beautiful love stories, Dr. Zhivago by Boris Pasternak, that he had read so many times. It was a love story set during the creation of the communist USSR, and the Officer was in his final year of high school when he read the book for the first time. Even after reading about one hundred pages, he could not understand what was going on. However, as the story developed, he immersed himself in the book and read it non-stop for hours together.

When he saw that movie with Dr. Iyenger, he remembered that both of them had a tough time containing their tears. They were overwhelmed with emotions. He was mesmerized by the acting and looks of Julie Christie, a celebrated Hollywood actress who played the heroine 'Lara' in the movie. Officer was so impressed with Dr. Zhivago's main character, played by Omar Sharif, that he almost identified the hero with his personality. By the end of the movie, Dr. Iyenger's head was on his shoulder, and he could feel the wetness of his T-shirt due to her tears.

It was June, and the Officer could feel the calm wind and smelt an identifiable fragrance in the air. Yes, it was the scent he loved. There was lavender growing nearby. Officer smiled as he messaged Reshma that he had landed in Moscow. He loved to share his all moments with Reshma. It gave him a strange sense of peace and happiness within. He could never pinpoint the reason, nor was he interested in dissecting the basis. He simply cherished that feeling. As a matter of routine, Officer's day ended every night by wishing Reshma 'good night' before retiring for the day.

His interpreter in Moscow was one beautiful young Russian lady. She introduced herself as Gorica. She had a honey red complexion on white skin. The unique color of skin one rarely saw. Her nose tip would turn red whenever the temperature dipped.

She was a single mother of two girls in love with a man seven years younger than her. She was a friendly, kind, and warm-hearted woman. Surprisingly she knew all four South Indian languages, including Sanskrit, Hindi, and English, and hence was one of the most sought-after interpreters. She owned a travel agency and would invariably give administrative and interpreter services to Government guests mainly from India. Whenever an Officer category guest came from India, she would herself try to attend to them. She was smitten with everything that was Indian. Her hero was Lord Krishna, from Bhagwad Geeta. Gorica was amazed by the way Krishna explained the essence of life to Arjuna.

She often wondered why Indians never invaded the world. She used to say, "They were capable of ruling the world with their spiritual powers and could have used some of those to bring peace to the world." She concluded from available ancient Indian literature that Indians as a race were more inclined to spiritual satisfaction than expansionism, unlike one of 'their' large neighbors. She felt that Indians believed in looking inward, and every action of theirs was directed towards attaining ' moksha' that was to come out of a cycle of numerous lives and deaths. She would read and re-read Bhagwad Geeta again and again and find deeper meaning through it every time.

After working hours, the Officer and Gorica would always grab some coffee and chat for a while. Before the day ended for her, she would have a few shots of vodka. One day she asked the Officer, "Do you believe in reincarnation ?" The Officer found that question so strange as it was a common belief for any typical Indian.

"Of course, I do, all Indians do, I mean all Hindus do." replied the Officer.

Tell me more requested Gorica. Her eyes gleamed as she downed her third shot. Officer appreciated her giving him company every day, but for Gorica, it was her chance to know more about Indian culture, traditions, etc. Officer was also delighted that someone would probably be impressed with his half-baked knowledge of spirituality because he was at the receiving end of all such knowledge until now. Officer thought - Swami Iyer would have laughed at him. SFO would have only wanted to know the Officer's plan to take Gorica to bed, and while Dr. Spike might have felt jealous of Gorica, she would possibly deny even that thought to herself. Anyway, the Officer was thrilled to explain whatever little he knew regarding the Indian beliefs.

Reincarnation

"Reincarnation, it simply means the rebirth of a soul in a new body. It's believed that death is not the end of a soul as every soul will be reborn; in a new body, in accordance with one's karmas." It was way beyond the Officer to explain the concept of karma.

Sensing that, Gorica smiled as she felt that she knew the concept much better than the Officer himself. She did know much more and told the Officer she would say to him her understanding. Gorica also learned much more than the Officer about his country's culture, traditions, etc. She had visited almost all places other than the northeastern states. Eventually, she wanted to settle either in Goa or in one of the ashrams of Rishikesh. She wanted to write a book explaining the true essence of Mahabharta.

She started by giving the Officer a background of herself. She told him that she was left alone with two small girls by her drunkard lover. She went into mild depression and started meditation. She learned various types of meditation; transcendental, mantra, zen, yoga, etc. Though the ways were different, so were the concepts, but the primary purpose was to look inward for spiritual enhancement.

She said that even though this might sound abstract to some people, it was true, and it went a long way in explaining a whole lot from soul mate to soul ties, etc. It was the reason why one would meet a lady or man for the first time, and it felt like they were 'old souls.' They felt as though they'd known each other before. She told the Officer that sometimes we do not realize that we've all had an experience when we meet someone for the first time and yet thoroughly cherish the time and conversation with them. Then, a few moments later, you feel like you can trust them even with your vast inner secrets. That's a reincarnated love soul right there.

Listening to this fascinating stuff from Gorica, the Officer remembered Reshma. He did not know why but he did have a contented smile. However, that day Officer had a different sort of feeling of fulfillment when he wished Reshma 'good night'. He wondered why he wanted to message only Reshma this 'good night' message – night after night. He just could not get an answer from his mind as to why he did not feel like wishing that to anyone else, even though he was part of so many groups and by now had so many friends.

Gorica had read all of Brian Weiss's books and was particularly impressed with 'Many Lives, Many Masters' as that book brought out reincarnation in great detail. While she talked, she would, at times, lightly pat the Officer on his back or place her hand on his thigh while conversing. The frequency of touch increased with the quantity of vodka inside her. Finally, she asked the Officer, "do you know how you can say or identify a person as your soul mate as being the one who has probably been reincarnated just to be with you?" The Officer was stunned by that question. His expression gave away his being lost. Gorcia then explained.

How to Know a Reincarnated Soulmate?

"Just like I said earlier, it is possible to meet a lover from your past life. Perhaps someone who came back to fulfill their love destiny in your life, or you guys were together, but things didn't end right. So, how do you know a reincarnated lover when you come in contact with one? Just for info, you know, I am still waiting for mine." Gorica laughed aloud.

Gorica was impressed at the depth of life that scriptures of Hinduism provided. She had read all major ones in Sanskrit and understood their essence more than many

Indians. So she told the Officer, let me tell you a little more:

Gut-Check

"Have you ever met someone and instantly liked the person? Like, you guys go on and talk for hours, and you just can't get to have enough? You may even forget to ask for their name, but it feels like you've known the person before. If you've experienced that, then it means it is probably someone from your past life. The same goes with instantly hating someone when you meet them without any reason. It could be you guys had an issue in the past life, or you just never liked the person then. Whatever the case is, when you feel an instant love or hatred for someone you just met for the first time, then they were probably people you knew in your other life."

Drawn to Each Other - Soulmates

"Another way to tell if someone is your soulmate from a past life is when you guys form a bond effortlessly. The truth is, nothing is a coincidence in this life. There is the reason you crossed paths with that person, and it could be because you guys were once together in the other life. Now, soulmates don't necessarily have to come to you in the form of a lover. In some cases, they could be some strange passerby who saved your life, your neighbor, your friend, or virtually anyone around you. They are only coming in contact with you now because, in the other life, it could be you guys had an unfinished business."

Officer wondered who in his life could be his soulmate. Dr. Iyenger, of course, was the one. He felt so complete with her. Was there anyone now? If he asked SFO, he knew SFO would tell him to forget about soulmate and just kiss Gorcia. SFO's only concern was that Indians should not be mistaken as non-romantics or lousy lovers by any woman in the world. His thought was that his country's image should stand out amongst all kinds of lovers!

However, for the Officer, he was now in deep thought as a 'soul searcher'. Gorcia had stirred his thinking such that only one face crossed his mind from his numerous connections and contacts, and that was of Reshma Kandwal. He had no romantic leaning towards her but wondered what their relationship was? He would often think. Friends? No.... Lovers....no no. They had not even met.

Role Play

Gorica had another shot of vodka and continued. "Now, here is a tricky one. Whether in a parent relationship or a lover's relationship, there are times where there seems to be a reversal in roles. A mother always being cared for by her daughter could mean that the daughter was the mother in another life. Even in a relationship, people start feeling like they are dads to their lovers, and this feeling is often accurate. If you often feel this reversal in roles while with a person, then the chances are that the person is from your past life."

Officer was convinced that Gorica could beat most of the Indian pandits hollow if they ever discussed these topics. She had so much clarity in her thoughts. She would often give references too. But, on the other hand, the Officer felt clueless about his own culture.

Time Seems to Fly

"Another sign that someone is from your past life is when your friendship with them feels like a lifetime. Whenever you are with them, all you will wish for is to have more time with them. Having their presence will never be enough for you, and you will always find yourself asking for more of their time. Why is that? Because whenever you're with them, you'll often feel like a complete puzzle. They'll often end your words for you, share thoughts with you, and everything will feel mutually yoked. If you have such a friendship, then such person is undoubtedly from your past life. You guys have known each other before; hence, the reason why time flies whenever you are with them."

"Time flies when I am with you too," retorted the Officer. Suddenly, Gorica, who had downed quite a few shots of vodka, did not say anything, but instead, she held the hand of the Officer and led him out of the bar towards a railing on the bank of river Moskva. She did not give him a chance to react and kissed him straight on his lips. When their lips met on that fantastic summer evening, it was as if the goddess of love had directed them how to kiss with passion never experienced before by humankind. It was like a transfer of honey into hot milk or molten lava flowing into the water. At that moment, time stood still. Gorica's luscious lips wanted more and more, and the Officer's passion matched hers on the lips, eyes, neck, and nose. When they disengaged, it was more than forty-five minutes that too only because Gorica was distracted by a phone call from her daughter. She had to leave as she was already delayed. Officer walked her up to her car. Both kissed again as if they were searching for their respective souls within each other. She smiled as she drove away.

Officer did not know whether he was delighted or sad at this new development. He called SFO. He could see SFO jumping with joy over the video call he had placed to narrate the incident. SFO cheered him from his home in Munger, a small town in Bihar. Officer requested SFO not to share this development with Dr. Spike or Swami Iyer. After promising the Officer that he would not, the first thing SFO did was send a message to Dr. Spike and Swami Iyer telling them of the incident. While Swami Iyer just shook his head, teardrops rolled on Dr. Spike's cheeks. Who knows whether Dr. Spike thought that Gorica finally enjoyed her passion and chance with the Officer. After all, Dr. Spike had convinced herself that the Officer, though so close to her, was her subject, and her only task or challenge was to bring the Officer to normalcy in the state of being himself, pre-Dr Iyenger's loss.

That day Officer did not send a good night message to Reshma. His hands just would not open the specific app he used to communicate his goodnight message to her.

162

He also felt that Dr. Iyenger was laughing aloud in front of him and was amused at the Officer kissing Gorica. It was as though she told him to go ahead with Gorica and make love to her as well. After all, the Officer was also now aware that Dr. Iyenger was also married when she met the Officer. Officer was shaken out of his thought process by the horn of a barge in river Moskva. He felt very uneasy at the thought of Dr. Iyenger. He also wondered how he would face Gorica the next day.

Fragmented souls

On the other side, after Gorica made her daughters comfortable in the bed, she tried hard to remember something told to her by one Hindu sage while she learned Sanskrit at Banaras. Banaras (or Varanasi), one of the oldest towns in India, also considered one of the holiest places in India, is a great learning place. Banaras was synonymous with Lord Shiva, a God of destruction and death. Banaras Hindu University has a great blend of modern, ancient, and spiritual education. Gorica was registered in the 'Sanskrit department.' Gorica recalled how the Sanskrit department would often invite revered sages to discuss ancient scriptures and life philosophy.

One such Sage that visited the Banaras university used to be in 'Tapasya'(or penance) most of the year. He was from an affluent family, educated in English literature from Oxford University, UK. One day he decided to go to the Himalayas to do Tapasya. Along the way, he met with other Sages with whom he held several discussions to enhance his spiritual knowledge. One particular Sage he met was a senior assistant to renowned Sage Shankracharya at Joshimath, near Badrinath Dham in Uttrakhand, in northern India. The visiting Sage lectured Gorica's class about debts of past lives and unfulfilled promises in the broader sense. She remembered sage's lecture was centered around the kinds of 'Souls.'

Gorica felt strange happiness as she recollected the events of the evening with the Officer. She recalled what the Sage had told her class, "Other than soul mates, we also have what is known as 'fragmented souls.' In the simplest of forms, fragmented souls are souls that have been willingly traded for something in return. For instance, selling your soul for fame, money, or power will result in a fragmented soul. The spiritual entity you've sold your soul to will take a fragment of your soul, sometimes a greater part, leaving you to be less whole. Other than this, nothing can ever happen to a person's soul. So, how does this affect love? If your soul is fragmented, perhaps because you traded part of your soul to a higher body in return for something, you'll hardly feel happy or content with your partner. It will affect your ability to love your partner, and most times, you'll often find yourself depressed. So, what can you do to avoid having a fragmented soul? First, steer clear from soul deals while alive. That way, your soul will be in one piece, and you'll enjoy life and love to the best of your ability."

Gorica was wondering. Was the evening all about lust or a case of fragmented soul of extreme loneliness? She rejected the idea of being lonely as many men would have given their right arm just to be with her. She would diplomatically stop advances from men. Her personality was such that she never got attracted to any typical sort of men, however handsome. For her, the man was first required to be on a higher spiritual plane even to get remotely interested in him. For being attracted to him, the man needed to have virtues that conformed with her own intellect. She found the Officer had a blend of everything that she loved.

She remembered Sage explaining.

Twin Flames

"Twin flames are people that you meet once in a lifetime. They are like a mirror of you, and the connection you have with them goes way deeper than what you'll have with your soulmate."

The sage explained that while the term soulmate is heard so often, the term twin flame is now coming into our collective consciousness more than ever. He went on to say the reason for that is more of these unions are occurring now. So, what is a twin flame connection, and how different is it from a soulmate connection? " The sage elaborated

Intensity

"One of the defining features that kind of stands out in terms of the difference between a twin flame connection and a soulmate connection is the 'intensity. We use the term a lot because we all know what a soulmate is. Thus, when we say you are my soulmate, it indicates a certain amount of intensity. Thereon, you'll start hearing things like this is the person I love, this is the person I'm going to marry and spend the rest of my life with. Why? Because they're my soul mate. The soul mate connection is a firm, definitely a solid romantic bond between two people. However, the Twin Flame connection is even stronger than the soulmate connection. The reason that it's so much more intense is that when you meet your twin flame, you're literally looking at yourself. The sage had earlier stated, your twin flame is sort of a fragment—the fragment of your soul. The twin flame connection is the strongest mirror of yourself that anyone can have in reality. So, it's so very intense. When you meet your twin flame, your life will never be the same from that point onward. It results in a very immediate and intense connection."

Purpose

Gorica remembered how she would be simply spellbound, especially whenever the sage lectured. She was the only foreigner in his class. She was brought up in the environment of the Russian Orthodox church, yet she was somehow more of a Hindu at heart. She wanted to learn as much as she could on the twin flame connection during her course in contrast to her classmates who would bunk classes to catch the first show of movie and enjoy evening frolics.

She recollected the sage saying:

"Though the twin flame connection can be very similar to a soulmate connection, the purpose is a little different. So while your soulmate can be your partner, the person you marry, the person that you come home to every day after a day of work, the person that gives you support, the person that's your shoulder that you cry on; of course, the kind of the general definition of the soulmate, the purpose of a twin flame is different.

The purpose of a twin flame connection has a lot to do with your mission in life, with what you're here to do. This can include your life's work. So, your twin flame will not only be your partner in the sense of it, but they will be your partner in completing your work. The work that you decided you want to do as a soul in this incarnation. So, twin flames will frequently have very similar missions in terms of what they want to work. Twin flames may work together like actually working together in partnership, either in businesses or other adventures. So that's how twin flame is a little bit different than a soulmate connection. "

Not as You'd Expect

"Unlike soulmate connection, twin flame union is a very unconventional relationship. If you meet your twin flame and expect that you're going to settle down, propose to them, marry, have a nice little house with a white picket fence, you're setting yourself up for a huge disappointment. If you're going to conform to this kind of standard of what a partnership means, you're in for a rude awakening because one of the purposes of a twin flame connection is to come in and establish a new paradigm for what relationships are. So, given this sense, a relationship is exactly what is normally understood by all: you settle down, you get married, and so on, Twin Flame connection is coming in to say, "Hey, we are here to redefine what a relationship can look like. Of course, it can continue to look like where you marry, have children, have a house together, and all of that, but this other form of living a relationship lets us show you. So, in a Twin Flames Union, the couple will show those around them a different way of perceiving a relationship because it would be very unconventional at times."

'Oh, Jesus,' that was the natural expression of Gorica whenever she was overwhelmed. It was like a journey towards the truth—the kind of truth she always wanted to explore.

She also remembered.

Evolution

"Another characteristic of a twin flame is that a twin flame is literally like a flame. It is your fast-track ticket to evolution, and what do I mean by this? When you meet your twin flame, your life will never be the same again, and literally, your twin flame is like a flame held to your feet constantly. They will be forcing you to evolve. Your twin flame is literally from the moment that you materialize in front of each other. Your twin flame will be burning things in you, burning patterns, subconscious beliefs, karma from past lives because the twin flame connection is ancient. So, as soon as that person materializes in front of you, they will begin to burn things that need to be burned in you. "

"Now, this fast-track ticket to evolution can be a little hard sometimes to live with. When twin flames meet, there is a pulling away a lot of times because the intensity is so high. The intensity in that connection is such that the flame is already burning things in you. Initially, you can feel or get scared because you will start to see things in you that need to change. You will now have this drive-in you wanting to be a better person that you want to evolve, and it's almost automatic. It's something that you have no control over. Transformation begins in you, and sometimes your mind has a little bit of a hard time catching up to that evolution because the evolution is occurring very quickly and outside of the control of your ego. Many times, the initial bonding of Twin Flames is a bit dramatic though they will be pulling away and re-approximation and pulling away and getting back. So, there's this dance of twin flames that occurs because of the intensity to fast track ticket to evolution."

Gorica tried hard to analyze her situation with whatever she had learned, but she felt more confused than ever. She was wide awake and was amazed at what one liplock could do to her. It was indeed not a very normal kiss. It was not a flow of spirituality but sort of a merger of souls as such. It was a sublime feeling. Officer was so innocent, courteous, intelligent, and such a handsome gentleman, and that too not from her country. He had struck the perfect chord in Gorcia. In few days, he would be gone to India. Then what would happen? All these questions were troubling Gorica. She got up and went to her small study room. From notes that she had made while conversing with the sage in India, she found a few pages that seemed like they were specially written for her. The topics were:

Bond Power

"Your twin flame can be across the world, but you are connected energetically. So, even when you're physically distant and time apart for months to years, it doesn't change the connection's intensity or strength. Your twin flame is a fragment of yourself in this incarnation, such that the link can't be broken. When you are together, it's a type of union that exerts such a strong influence on people around you that everyone notices there's something between you two, even though that person may not be spiritual. Someone could just look at you and easily decipher guys being connected, even though they are not spiritual or knowledgeable in these aspects. They can perceive the strength of the connection between two individuals with ease. So, twin flames have an indestructible bond that can easily be detected."

Constructive or Destructive

"Since twin flame relationships are so powerful, they have the potential to be constructive or destructive. Perhaps the reason that more Twin Flames is incarnating in this lifetime. It wasn't always this way. Usually, before this era, one of the Twin Flames stayed on the other side and served as a guide to the twin flame that was in. Why? Because the strength of the bond is so intense that if both Twin Flames incarnated in the same lifetime, the potential for destruction was high. So, in this era, because the energy is intense, our evolution of consciousness is exploding. Our evolution of consciousness is more now open to Twin Flames incarnating in the same lifetime. Many people are finding their Twin Flames in this lifetime, and it's very beautiful. However, they need to be careful not to overstep boundaries as the intensity can be devastating. It's a very beautiful connection but it is a connection that can either be constructive or destructive. It all depends on how you perceive the connection, how you live through it, and the things that you allow to fall in terms of subconscious beliefs and attachments."

The next day Gorica shared all these aspects with the Officer. They walked on a passage on the side of Red Square at the end of the day. This time they were holding hands, and Gorica would lift his hand every now to kiss it intermittently.

The Officer wondered who were his Soulmates and who were his probable Twin flames. The choices of the latter were amongst Dr. Spike, Gorica, and Reshma. SFO and Swami Iyer were indeed his soulmates, and so was his wife. However, his thought process was breaking whenever Gorica lovingly brushed herself against the Officer's arm. He was getting aroused. She occasionally tightened the grip with which she held his hand in hers. She then talked about other aspects she had read in her notes.

Union

"There can't be the union of Twin Flames in this lifetime unless there is wholeness in each of the elements of the association. In the Twin Flame connection, you will not partner with your twin flame unless you are whole and your partner is whole; your twin flame is whole. So, what will happen is until you both enter a position of wholeness, you will be repelling each other in a certain way. The connection will repel itself unless the two elements are whole. You can meet your twin flame, and it can take years for the union to occur because there's so much work (unlike with soulmates) that needs to happen in you to become whole or to feel complete. The same for your twin flame."

She continued to talk.

Signs you've found your twin flame

"Before you even start to think of finding your twin flames, you need to understand the difference between soulmates and Twin Flames. Why? Because there are actually two completely different things, and it's essential to know the differences. Soul mates might be perfect matches, but Twin Flames are our complete mirrors. In other words, they complete us in a much more accurate sense compared to soul mates. Opposites attract, after all, there are other halves, and these relationships are usually roller coasters of emotion where you might be patient. Your twin flame may get antsy, and where you're more to yourself, your twin flame may be very social. Quite the opposite of what you are, like a missing piece in a puzzle."

They Complete You

"Do you feel that your partner brings out the best in you? Do you feel most fulfilled when you're around them? If you only feel like you're whole when you're with your partner, there's a good chance that it's your twin flame. According to an ancient Greek story by Plato, people originally had four legs and arms plus a head with two faces. At some point, these early humans were separated into two halves. Now, this interesting fictional story perfectly illustrates what Twin Flames are all about. They're your long-lost other halves that are meant to complete you."

By now, both the Officer and Gorica were indeed burning with internal desires. Gorica's daughters were on a weekend school camp away from Moscow. It did not take long for them to reach Gorcia's house and get cozy! After Officer and Gorica were through with passionate lovemaking and lay in each other's arms, she whispered in his ears, " You complete me. You have given me a feeling of completeness today!" Gorica's smile was heavenly, like her well-sculptured figure. She then lit a cigarette.

Officer wondered if they were twin flames. He had thoroughly enjoyed making love to Gorica but somehow did not find the completeness he used to feel with Dr. Iyenger. He did not want to compare, as the two relationships were entirely different. Gorica told him that she knew that their relationship was temporary and there was no way to bring permanence. All she wanted was a promise from the Officer that he would spend his time with her whenever he was in Moscow. That was not a difficult promise for the Officer.

That weekend was like a fabulous dream that finished so fast. Officer and Gorica were together all the time. Officer had a great quest for knowledge, and Gorica was too ready to oblige. They spent time enjoying local wine, eating rye bread, boiled potatoes, but most of all making passionate love several times. They discussed Kamsutra, a great work by Vatsyayana, and marvel at that text's contents and presentation. The ultimate and practical book written on love and sex.

When the Officer got back to his hotel, he promptly narrated the weekend's events to SFO, again with the condition that SFO would not tell anyone. However, post their conversation, the first action of SFO was to send a mail to Dr. Spike and Swami Iyer. Swami Iyer would always scratch his head in disgust, while Dr. Spike would not comment or show expression but probably held back her emotions with some regret. SFO would always pour himself a stiff peg of rum, light his obnoxious-smelling cigarette, and reminisce whatever the Officer had told him, primarily his actions that involved making love.

Officer was still not at peace. He still was looking for answers! What still made him sad was why Dr. Iyenger hid her marriage from him. What was there in Dr. Iyenger that connected him so profoundly with her? Why was her smiling face not going away from his mind even after so many years of her plane crash?

His hands trembled when he sent his regular 'Good night' message to Reshma. Yet, he wondered why that sending that two-lettered message gave him so much solace and satisfaction. He had not even met her. When they did chat, he would share all his life's details with her. He felt that she was the most caring person he had come across in his life so far. She also found him very loving, caring, highly respectful, and full of love. She would also share a lot with him.

On the other hand, she felt embarrassed at times and would not open up fully. She was not very expressive in writing but had a treasure of WhatsApp forwards to convey what she wanted. Somehow, the Officer understood everything: her emotions, fears, likings, and dislikes, even without speaking to her. That was strange, and probably both of them knew that. They would talk on the phone very rarely. However, it was enough to transcend the Officer into a different universe. He was

175

convinced that there were many universes, in accordance with the modern theory of the multiverse, and out of that, one belonged to only Reshma and him. It was a strange feeling that he had never ever felt with anyone.

Was Reshma his twin flame? He always wondered and hoped like hell that it was true. So he wished to know more and more on the subject. Her vivaciousness, grace, elegance enamoured him, and he always felt that she would be wearing the lavender-based perfume even without having met her once. Her voice was music to his ears.

By now, the Officer and Gorica were completely comfortable with each other, and making love was a norm every time she came over to his hotel. After making love, Officer always requested Gorica to tell him more of what she had learned. Of course, she was more than willing to oblige.

Feel Like You've Known Them Your Whole Life

"Meeting your twin flame for the first time can be a strange yet familiar experience. Some lovers even have a feeling of Deja vu as if the encounter had happened before. On the other hand, maybe you've met your twin flame before in a past life. Whatever the reason, Twin Flames feel like they've known each other for their entire lives. Even when they meet for the first time, you know each other better than anyone else. While soulmates are sometimes referred to as part of your spiritual family, Twin Flames hold even more meaning. You know each other on an intense level, more so than any of your family members or close friends. Twin Flames; they're the only people in the world who completely understand one another."

Learn Together

"Twin Flames are completely intrigued by each other and not just because of physical or romantic attraction. With each passing day you spend with your twin flame, you learn something completely new, and these lessons help you grow as a person more so than you ever thought possible. This is one of the many things which keep Twin Flames so magnetically attracted since the experiences are shared with someone important to you. As a result, they hold that much more value."

As Gorica was explaining these aspects, the Officer's mind was levitating with thoughts of love for Dr. Iyenger. That made him kind of sad. However, his thoughts were suddenly diverted towards Reshma Kandwal, and he felt energized as pleasant thoughts of Reshma were overpowering and uplifting his mood out of that sadness. It actually made him feel better.

For Gorica, the ecstatic feeling that she derived from making love with the Officer was one of ultimate bliss in the universe that soaked her with satisfaction. Her encounter with the Officer was emotionally, physically, and spiritually fulfilling. She did not want her time with the Officer to end, but there was little they could do, as he was slated to fly out on the coming Monday evening. She thought about sage's golden words and repeated them to the Officer.

You Don't Hold Back Your Emotions When You're Together

"When you're with your twin flame, you feel completely vulnerable. There's no point in putting up walls or pretending to be someone you're not. Your twin flame will see right through this facade, so the only choice is to completely surrender to your emotions and each other. However, this isn't a negative thing as Twin Flames find themselves craving this sense of ability."

They Help You Confront Your Fears

"Twin Flames are inseparably in love partly because they help each other conquer their fears. Now, as nice as this sounds, it's not necessarily a pleasant process. However, it's a much-needed experience to grow. Twin Flames force each other to stare deep into the dark, scary abyss of their souls. This drags many intense and painful emotions to the surface that are difficult but are needed to mature."

It's Anything but Boring If You Find Your Twin Flame

"You're in for one hell of a ride. Being with your twin flame isn't necessarily fun because you might argue, break up and cry endless tears together. However, be prepared for a lot of ups and downs as your twin flame forces you to confront the most intense emotions you'll ever feel in your entire life. However, twin flames have an intensely and insanely strong impact on each other's lives. An impact as strong as an asteroid slamming into Earth."

You'll Always Forgive Each Other Unconditionally

"Even though you might get into extremely passionate arguments with your twin flame, you'll always find yourself forgiving them unconditionally. Try as you might; it's impossible to shut them out of your lives completely, and because you know each other so well, you ultimately understand why certain decisions were made even if they caused you pain. But, as a life partner, they should be willing to recognize that they hurt you and work with you to make sure it doesn't happen consistently."

So so so true. Officer was getting more and more convinced that he and Reshma do have a similar bond. Whether they were twin flames or not was a matter that needed further clarity. Dr. Iyenger was indeed his twin flame. He was sure about it. But then why did she have to die so young? Officer was angry with the only entity, and that was God. Why did God have to take Dr. Iyenger away at such an early age?

Gorica hugged and kissed him Goodbye as she dropped him off at the railway station so that he could catch the Airport Express train that would take him to

Sheremetyevo International airport. Officer kissed her, too, as his heart filled up with a bit of emotion for all the intimate time he had with her. He promised that he would return to Moscow at the first opportunity.

As he waited in the lounge, he messaged Reshma that Moscow airport was one of the worst airports in the world and smiled. He again realized that he simply could not help sharing everything with Reshma. He then realized it was around 2215 hrs in India. So he smiled and messaged, ' Good Night, Take Care' and poured single malt whisky for himself as he watched a football match between Brazil and Germany on TV at the lounge. He felt nice when he saw Reshma's return message. ' GN, you too, TC.' Even though a short message, the Officer looked at it a couple of times and smiled, thinking they hadn't even met he felt a 'loving' connection.

IX
Manifesting Love and happiness

*"What you think you become. What you feel you
attract. What you imagine you create."*

Budha

By now, the Officer was armed with so much
knowledge about love and its relationships, various
forms, Psychology, astrology, mystery, and many more
aspects. However, it was still not clear how one
manifested love.

With the influence of Dr. Spike, he had learned to
research the subject. Likewise, swami Iyer was
instrumental in his spiritual growth. He recalled that
both believed that love was the most profound spiritual
phenomenon encompassing past lives, Psychology,
conscious and subconscious minds, etc.

Dr. Spike's own life had undergone an incredible
metamorphosis when she decided to get married to SFO.
She accepted his proposal even though he smoked that
obnoxious brand of cigarettes with an equally foul smell.
She laughed when he proposed to her, but having spent
a long night with him, they talked and made love all
night. She felt she connected with him from within. It
was a matter of minutes when she hugged him and said
yes! She knew and felt that he had a heart of gold, was a
genuinely caring person, and would always make her

happy. They were married in a temple of Darbhanga not far from his house. On a special request from the Govt of Bihar, she agreed to work there for three months every year at Lalit Narayan Mithila University at Darbhanga as a visiting Professor. With the passage of time, SFO and she had a lovely boy. Her child with SFO and her older daughter made a beautiful family with a combination of dark and white skins. SFO would narrate stories of his extensive sea experiences to his stepdaughter. One day while telling her some story, she commented on the disgusting smell emanating from his mouth. Without blinking an eyelid, he chucked the packet of remaining cigarettes in the trash and never touched any form of tobacco again.

Meanwhile, Dr. Spike was amazed at the kind of love she felt in a spiritually rich India with so much cultural diversity. She especially admired the loving, respectful, and caring relationship that most children showered towards their parents. Whenever Dr. Spike returned to the University in Oslo, SFO was too happy to accompany her and spend the rest of the year in Oslo. SFO and Dr. Spike had still not forgotten their resolve to ensure that they would work towards getting the Officer's state of mind to pre-Dr Iyenger's incident.

Officer's Dilemma

In the meantime, the Officer developed a habit of voracious reading. He was particularly impressed with the works of Brian Weiss and read all his books, as Gorica had also talked highly of him. He was fascinated to read Rhonda Byrne's 'Secret ' and ' The Magic.' He wanted to learn how to practice creative visualization, gratitude, scripting, affirmations, incantations, self-hypnosis, NLP, etc. When he read Naville Godard, the Officer was in a different world. He was genuinely amazed and wanted to practice and see whether imagination with emotions could manifest.

Introduction to Life Coaching

He did not know how to do that. Since he was inquisitive by nature, he started following many experts on 'youtube channels.' There were countless experts, and the Officer would patiently hear them and then eliminate and select those who appealed to him. They were popularly known as 'Life Coaches' and had been doing great jobs in coaching people to manifest love, make money, and ensure good health. The sky was the limit of what one could display or achieve with the techniques perfected by these life coaches.

Great Life Coaches coaches used a 'pull system' to help you manifest what you desired the most. They made you work rather than spoon-feeding in accordance with your aspirations, happiness parameters and ensure that one manifests greater self-esteem, confidence, higher vibrations so essential for manifestation of your desires. That, in turn, enhanced one's happiness, enjoyment index, increased energy levels, and lowered stress levels.

According to Rhonda Byrne, who uncovered the secret of life, as the Law of Attraction, conveyed that our current thoughts create our future. Therefore, what we thought with emotions, coupled with gratitude, manifested in our life.

Sheena Shah and Law of Attraction

Officer found out that one of the best life coaches in the world was a lady named Ms. Sheena Shah. She was a Law of Attraction Life Coach. She was based out of Mumbai and would often travel all over the world. Her favourite cities were Vienna and Budapest. She believed that Venice was more of a hype. However, the nature of her job allowed her to work from any location globally as most interactions were possible online.

She was beautiful to look at, her face had an aura of kindness, and her mannerism would make anyone most comfortable. She patiently listened to the Officer and diagnosed that Officer needed to manifest love. He needed help and coaching. He also needed to give attention to his career and have explicit goals chalked out to live his life happily.

When the Officer discussed this with Dr. Spike, she was also convinced that the Officer needed a life coach. SFO, too agreed, especially after having learned that Sheena Shah was gorgeous to look at. Officer's birthday was approaching, and Dr. Spike informed the Officer that she would gift him these life coaching sessions. Officer was overwhelmed with joy and gratitude as Sheena Shah's services were indeed very expensive.

Sheena Shah fixed an appointment after two weeks and conveyed that she would be taking six sessions of one hour each on Skype at staggered intervals lasting over a couple of weeks.

Simply put, the law of Attraction simply meant that you attract what you think and what you are, and Sheena had indeed mastered the art of imparting this knowledge.

Affirmations and Self Love

At the onset, she told him to breath in and breath out three times, counting one to four as he breathed in, then holding his breath for four counts and breathing out for four counts. That was called box breathing. She explained to the Officer that we use only eight percent of the conscious mind and do not use the rest ninety-two percent of the subconscious mind. Therefore, our habits, personality, character, etc., were formed due to the subconscious programming as we grew up and nurtured in various environments, notwithstanding some inherited traits.

It was possible to program our minds with the help of affirmations. In simple words, affirmations are suggestions when used with the right words and right time straightway go to our subconscious mind and program subconscious mind accordingly. The best recommended time to say these affirmations to yourself was within half an hour window of getting up in the morning and before sleeping at night. Sheena told the Officer that self-love was the most important trait required to be taught and suggested that ten affirmations be practiced morning and night. She also coached the Officer by telling him basics like he could use any positive words after "I am......" for example, "I am healthy and fine" and "I am more than enough the way I am."

Officer could feel a sense of satisfaction and joy as he practiced whatever was taught every day. She had humorously warned him that affirmation "I am magnetic, I attract all those who matter to me, those who love me and like me" would attract many towards him. The Officer decided to give this a try, and he was amazed at the results. He suddenly started getting many more friend requests on social media. Got connected to many old friends that he never expected. There was this classmate of his who even confessed her infatuation she had for the Officer 35 years ago while they were in Kindergarten. Both laughed.

Visualisation Vibrations and Scripting

The results had started showing within few days of commencement of coaching. He was amazed at the topics covered from the second session onwards. Sheena began with coaching on affirmations with 'We are....' As a natural transition from 'I am.....'.

Officer simply loved it when Sheena exhorted upon the Officer never to use words like try, hope, wish, need, and want. These words denoted negativity.

We must ask the universe like a small child, with full right. We must never plead as it is our right to seek abundance and love. The challenge was 'how to.' That's where the role of the Coach becomes essential.

Sheena taught the Officer various kinds of meditations. There was nothing religious, but the Officer was always very spiritual as he was being trained to look inwards.

He was impressed by many quotes he would read on the Law of Attraction groups on FB. He learned that our intentions create our reality. How and why we must never 'Want' anything but should always believe that we 'Have' that or what we wish to have. With some techniques, it was possible to set goals and train ourselves to automatically manifest our desires. Some experts called that technique ' living in the end. Sheena was a tough taskmaster who would give lots of homework.

She coached the Officer well. She made him realize that there was so much power in whatever we focus our energy into. If one were so focused on being a positive person, they would be positive. That would be your reality. So, wherever your focus is, that's what would become your reality. Now, while trying to manifest happiness, you should never focus on things that may bring you sadness or depression over time. Now that was the key.

Officer confided in Sheena that he was unable to come out of Dr. Iyenger's incident. He did not have the heart to share this life coaching lesson with Reshma, as he wasn't sure of her reaction. However, he continued to share his learnings with Dr. Spike. The officer laughed at the fact that SFO was not urging him to make a pass at his life coach anymore. It was a definite change that Dr. Spike had brought about in the thinking of SFO. When he said that to SFO, they both laughed aloud.

Sheena told the Officer that we all are connected through microcosmic networking. Our existence is identical to the universe as a whole, and the universe is similar to our existence. We all were not bodies, but energy gets merged and connected. That amalgamation decides our bonds—the quality of bonds popularly known as relationships.

When the Officer complimented Sheena on her looks and pleasing personality, she reciprocated by saying that everyone was 'you' pushed out! She meant that the beauty that we see in others was actually what's inside us. Hence we needed to enrich ourselves internally. First, we should be saturated with love. Only then can we give it to others. A great point Officer learned. Each individual human life is a microcosm of life in the universe. Only earnestness of purpose is required.

He smiled. No wonder he was so differently attached to Reshma. Meditation was one way to live on a higher plane. It increased your vibrations, reduced anxiety, and kept you healthy, calm, and spiritually prosperous from inside.

Meditation

The lesson was to practice meditation regularly, as this was the only way to peace with your inner self. Once you were peaceful within, you would become more relaxed and happy. So, no matter how tight your weekly schedule often goes, always slot in a time for meditation.

How to Manifest

To manifest abundance in love, success, emotions, money, and exams, self-love was essential. Affirmations, visualization, and scripting were some very simple and great techniques to achieve that. When one is saturated with self-love, they were very confident and never insecure and exuded those qualities outside themselves. As a result, they would attract all kinds of success in a natural fashion. Self-love was very different from narcissism and ego.

Sheena Shah explained, "Start by loving yourself, which means love every ounce of who you are. Your limiting beliefs will distract you from being your highest self and being your higher power. It's now time to get rid of those". She continued, "I'm going to guide you through this process of how to get rid of those. Understand that loving yourself sets the tone for everything in your life. Everything in life was magnetic when it comes to energy. Hence, for you to be energetically aligned with the outcome, with the source of love, you have to connect with love, and love has to come from within because it's going to embrace everything around you if it comes from within is magnetic. The energy just comes

189

back to you. So, any self-limiting beliefs that you have are going to come back and bite you. So get rid of all of them. Start understanding that you are perfect the way that you are. There's no such thing as perfect shape, height, complexion, etc. Stop comparing yourself. Stop doing those things to idolize other people. Instead, start enjoying who you are right now. By doing that, I want to make you aware of some practices you can do to help yourself. The first way to loving yourself is to write down in a journal some things about yourself. Have that self-dialog, inner talk about yourself of how much you l Like I am affirmations that you are doing daily."

Gratitude

Sheena explained to the Officer that gratitude is one of the most powerful virtues in the universe. She told him the amazing truth that those who practiced gratitude manifest more and much faster. That was key to abundance. Therefore, practicing 'Gratitude' must be part of one's natural routine. For example, one could commence simply by thanking the universe as opening their eyes in the morning to see another day.

28 Days Plan

Sheena created a 28-day program for the Officer to follow the practice of Gratitude and many other techniques perfected by her to practice the Law of Attraction. Prominent amongst those were the water technique by which you transfer your thoughts with water, quantum jump for faster manifestation, and very effective techniques for building confidence, negativity removal, congratulatory technique, telephone message receiving technique, and many more. The underlying principle was visualization, scripting, emotions, raising vibrations, practicing gratitude for health, money, material and, non-material possessions, combined with affirmations and incantations. Incantations were special words spoken in a low tone to program the subconscious mind.

At the end of 28 days, Officer profusely thanked Sheena Shah. He was overwhelmed with gratitude and love. He was much more confident. He was feeling complete. He sent a bouquette of flowers to Sheena Shah, his life coach who had transformed the Officer somehow, and he was set to gain new heights once again.

The first time he thought about Dr. Iyenger without feeling low. He felt as if he was cherishing her great memories. He remembered Swami Iyer telling him the meaning of a verse from revered Garud Puran that no amount of crying would get the dead back. They were already on their next journey. Officer started to understand that more than ever before. He did feel the void, but it was minuscule.

That day when he sent a regular 'GN' message to Reshma, there was a happy underlying tone of a different kind, intermingled with sublime contentment and relief. Reshma always understood these underlying sentiments and would send an emoji of a smile when she replied.

191

SFO, Swami Iyer, and Dr. Spike were more than convinced that their efforts, coupled with the Officer's own internal desire and efforts, were instrumental in his highly reduced melancholy. However, they were blissfully not aware of Reshma in his life.

Post his annual leave, the Officer was asked to proceed to Ladakh, a Union Territory in northern Himalayas, bordering Tibet for some inter-services discussions at ground level on the issue of deployment at Pangong Tso lake. This vast saltwater lake was about one-third in Indian and two-thirds in Chinese territory and was disputed between the two countries.

As usual, the Officer shared this news with Reshma. Then, he slept with a smile as Reshma replied, " Rest properly, TC."

X
The Fateful Day

"One day, the Universe will bless you with one person that gives you everything you've ever prayed and cried for in other people. And it will be beautiful."

Unknown Author

Pangong Tso Lake

As the Officer walked out of the exit gate of Kushok Bakula Rimpochee Airport at Leh, capital of Ladakh, he turned around to see who had tapped him on his shoulder. He could not believe his eyes when he saw the lady who had tapped his shoulder and was giggling at him so dotingly was none other than Reshma. He was stunned beyond words, he was speechless, and his heart was pounding with joy. The sparkle that he saw in the eyes of Reshma was actually in his eyes too. She was stunningly beautiful, and he could tell how happy she was too in seeing the Officer. He wondered whether he was in Utopia or was it a reality? All he could do was to exclaim loudly, Oh My God, finally! Oh My God!' Then, both of them laughed aloud and looked at each other with the most adoring eyes.

Reshma informed him that she was there with her three colleagues to study art and craft in five villages of that area. She said that she was there on behalf of an NGO to promote the art of those hill villages of the Himalayan region in other parts of the country. She told him that

193

their schedule was not so busy as such. Officer asked Reshma and her group to wait as he wanted to check his own schedule. He discussed the next day's plan with his liaison Officer. He told Reshma that he was headed to Pangong Tso lake for work the next day, and if Reshma and her group wanted, he would gladly take them along. He said the plan was to depart in the morning and return by night. The group was too happy with the offer, as it was not easy to visit those areas independently. Luckily, Reshma and her group's hotel was on the way to the lake and not far from the Officer's Mess where the Officer was staying.

It was going to be an arduous journey to the lake that would take about six hours, not because it was far but because the roads were not in the best condition. At 0500 hrs in the morning, the Officer reached the hotel where Reshma and her group stayed. When he saw all of them waiting, he signalled to Reshma to come and sit beside him in the front seat of the Jeep. Within no time of Reshma sitting next to him, the Officer could smell the fragrance of lavender. He thought to himself, "Is this coincidence, or was this meant to be?" It reminded him of Dr. Iyenger. However, this time he was not sad or lost in thought, but instead, he smiled as he remembered their drives on his bike. He was somehow convinced that Reshma was part of him. She smiled now and then, with so much affection and care in her eyes, every time their eyes met. As he drove, she narrated so many stories. He was not interested at all. He only wanted to hear her melodious voice in his ears. The group sang and laughed as he drove. Some even took a quick nap after enjoying the packed sandwiches the Officer had asked his mess staff to pack for the trip. On reaching the lake, the Officer went for his meeting at the Army outpost, while the group enjoyed their time at the lake, clicking pictures and having fun. As soon as his work was done, they headed back. Again, the Officer made sure that Reshma sat in front and beside him. While she continued to talk, he listened but was mainly enjoying her presence next to him. Somehow even the Officer could also sense that Reshma, too, felt similar emotions of love, respect, care, and awe as they sat next to each other during the drive. Most of all, the feeling of actual physical closeness was overwhelming for both of them. Both did not want that journey to end but then who could stop time.

As the Officer dropped off Reshma and her friends, he shook hands with Reshma. It was a kind of prolonged handshake. He instantly felt the transfer of energies along with the fragrance of lavender that he was so appealing.

"Your handshake gave me so much warmth and a beautiful feeling of closeness," Reshma replied to the Officer's 'good night' message. Officer could not comprehend the feelings that were also going through him. So he searched for a pen in his laptop bag, took out a plain paper, and commenced to write about his feelings.

When the Officer told Dr. Spike about his day, she was the happiest as she felt her subject had attained the ultimate bliss of happiness. He had experienced peace like Gautam Buddha. She could sense that even though the Officer and Reshma lived their lives at different places, their energies were flowing and had intermingled beautifully. There was a little requirement to meet physically as their bond was much beyond that. Their souls were too happy and satisfied to find each other. It was the most beautiful and sublime connection.

Swami Iyer was also writing his thoughts and believed Dr. Spike was right. SFO did think briefly about when the Officer and Reshma would get more intimate but never expressed it aloud. Gorica Rezaeva was probably the only one who knew that the Officer and Reshma were already in their own universe. They would meet birth after birth till they attain 'moksha.' Mankind would take many years before reaching that understanding.

XI
Epilogue – The Ultimate reality

"Whatever happened, happened for good, Whatever is happening, is happening for good. Whatever will happen will also happen for good."

Bhagavad Gita

Officer was filled with tears of joy and contentment as he began writing a letter. Handwritten notes or letters have gotten more and more rare, especially with younger generations. In the past, he had only written to Dr. Iyenger. In fact, he had written a letter to her a few days before her death. He could not remember what he wrote in that letter. He was now writing to Reshma and brimming with happiness, emotion, and a host of other indescribable feelings. The tears he was experiencing were of joy and a sort of fulfillment in his life. He had felt a strange sense of tranquility when he shook hands with Reshma. At that moment, he could not decipher how one could be so peaceful just by meeting someone for the first time.

The Officer then remembered concepts of soulmates, twin flames, and he knew for sure that Reshma was Dr.Iyengar's twin flame. Dr. Iyenger and Reshma were actually the same. Two bodies, fragments of the same soul. Pandit Naveen Parashar of Hoshiarpur's words, who read from Bhrigu Sanhita years ago, also clearly echoed in Officer's ears. The Officer and Reshma were two souls who had become one without anyone realizing that. It's just that they resided in two bodies. Officer was convinced.

Reshma obviously never knew about these concepts. All she understood was that their magnetic attraction was so difficult to explain but easy to feel. However, she did feel something extraordinary purely based on their connection, even when there were no expectations. There was no need to explain to anyone, and they both realised that. They were content in their own exclusive universe.

The Officer decided to narrate his story with Dr. Iyenger to Reshma. She heard the story with great compassion. After he narrated the story on the phone to Reshma, he suddenly noticed that handwritten letter that he had written to Reshma many years ago popping out through a folder in his bag. He had kept it safe, and even though it was in his bag, he never saw the letter as such after writing it.

The next day the Officer mentioned the letter to Reshma through a Whatsapp message. He told her that he had written a letter to her but never shared it with her. "I wish to read it," demanded Reshma. The Officer scanned those pages and sent them to her. Reshma was stunned. She felt something churned in her stomach. She understood and felt that there indeed was a unique bond and deep-rooted connection between the Officer and her. She was a lady who did not write much but had good comprehensive ability. Expressing the core of her heart, she wrote back one word, "Speechless," on WhatsApp to the Officer. Officer knew the depth of the word. As he continued to glance at the one-word reply, he could feel her touch and also somehow smell the fragrance of fresh Lavender flowers. He smiled and wrote his 'Goodnight' along with a sticker of a man kissing the forehead of his lady love with great affection and care.

He recollected the short lines from their messages, smiled, and said...."Please say Reshma...Please say...

"A cartoon like me
A fool like me
Apne number banane ki zaroorat nahi (Don't try to impress me)
I know better about myself
Ha ha ha......
No need to be smart
This time not possible
I am a normal person who knows nothing.
Some people think their wives are devils
No one knows me
Jhagda ho jayega (A misunderstanding might happen)
Agar gussa ho gayee tou aap manna Lena (If I ever get angry, make sure you cajole me)
As such
I will try
He he
Relax
Don't think so much
I feel awkward
You are impossible at times
Your handshake gave so much of warmth and nice feeling"

All he could hear was her enigmatic, musical, and loving voice whispering in his ears, " apne number banane kee zaroorat nahi." In summary, she meant: don't try to impress me, as she was already a part of him, they were one and would remain one, birth after birth, till they would be out of the bondage of life and death.

Of all the universes created by supreme power, theirs was unique and special. The Officer was now a most satisfied person with nothing bothering him anymore since he was content with the love and deep connection he had formed with Reshma. They had "Manifested Love."

References

- **An Epic – Mahabharta, 1947, Indian Press Ltd, Prayag.**
- **Rhonda Byrnes, 2006, Secret**
- **Rhonda Byrnes, 2012 The Magic**
- **Neville Godard, 1944, Feeling is the Secret**
- **Shankar Barua, 1995, The Art of Kamasutra, Richard Blady Publishing, London.**
- https://streamonlinefreemovies.com/psychological-facts-about-love
- https://www.ncbi.nlm.nih.gov/pmc/articles/PMC3277362/
- https://time.com/5321262/science-behind-happy-healthy-relationships/
- https://www.health.harvard.edu/mental-health/can-relationships-boost-longevity-and-well-being
- https://www.goodreads.com/quotes/433397-according-to-greek-mythology-humans-were-originally-created-with-four
- https://edition.cnn.com/travel/article/fall-in-love-airplane/index.html
- https://www.sciencedaily.com/releases/2013/02/130213093220.htm
- https://en.wikipedia.org/wiki/Personality_Psychology
- https://www.verywellmind.com/theories-of-love-2795341
- https://www.cleverism.com/Psychology-of-love/

- https://www.google.com/amp/s/www.refinery29.com/amp/en-us/love-stories-real-couples
- https://www.lifehack.org/584341/real-life-love-stories-that-will-remind-you-true-love-does-exist
- https://www.oprahdaily.com/life/relationships-love/a30472782/true-romantic-stories/
- https://www.google.com/amp/s/www.realsimple.com/work-life/family/relationships/love-stories%3famp=true
- www.loveandcrumb.com
- https://in.pinterest.com/pin/760615824548333138
- https://quotesdiary06.com
- https://yourquotes.in
- https://www.lifeinvedas.com
- https://www.quotesgram.com
- https://www.spiritbutton.com
- https://www.usurnsonline.com